Green Finance and Investment



# Developing Sustainable Finance Definitions and Taxonomies

OECD
BETTER POLICIES FOR BETTER LIVES

**Please cite this publication as:**
OECD (2020), *Developing Sustainable Finance Definitions and Taxonomies*, Green Finance and Investment, OECD Publishing, Paris, *https://doi.org/10.1787/134a2dbe-en*.

ISBN 978-92-64-51730-1 (print)
ISBN 978-92-64-97779-2 (pdf)

Green Finance and Investment
ISSN 2409-0336 (print)
ISSN 2409-0344 (online)

**Photo credits:** Cover © Kostiantyn/Shutterstock.com.

Corrigenda to publications may be found on line at: *www.oecd.org/about/publishing/corrigenda.htm*.

# Foreword

This report aims to provide policy makers with information and preliminary policy considerations in the emerging field of official definitions of sustainable finance. It examines the recently adopted EU Regulation on the establishment of a framework to facilitate sustainable investment (the "EU taxonomy"), as well as official definitions of sustainable finance in Japan, China, France and the Netherlands. It maps similarities in the coverage of certain economic sectors, such as renewable energy. It also identifies differences, in sector coverage but also in terms of approaches in principle to defining what it sustainable. [For instance, the EU regulation stands out in its combined approach of several environmental objectives, with a substantial contribution to one objective such as climate mitigation joined with a no significant harm requirement for other environmental objectives such as adaptation and other natural capital objectives]. It provides details of the frameworks that each of the above jurisdictions adopted in terms of official definitions of sustainable finance.

As finance is making further forays in the areas of sustainable investing and more recently in green recovery stimulus packages, investors have been seeking more clarity on how sustainable investments is defined. The report argues that some benefits can be brought to the market, including increasing investor confidence and market integrity, by having clearer definitions of sustainable finance. It also points to some elements of good practice in designing such definitions, including the necessity to be consistent with national climate objectives and pathways, and taking a system view in the design of principles, metrics and thresholds for identifying sustainable investments.

Developed by the Secretariat for the Working Party on Climate Investment and Development of the Environmental Policy Committee, the report has benefitted from the observer role of the OECD in the Technical Expert Group on Sustainable Finance of the European Commission. The group worked for two years on developing the detailed screening criteria for sustainable economic activities that were proposed to the Commission as a basis of the Delegated Act of the EU Taxonomy regulation, adopted in June 2020. The Environment Directorate of the OECD was pleased to be able to contribute its environmental expertise to the work of this group. Going forward, the OECD sits as an observer in the Platforms established by the EU to pursue the domestic development and international dialogue on taxonomies.

Dialogue across governments, and between public and private finance institutions, including multilateral organisations, is of paramount importance to facilitate the emergence of definitions of sustainable finance that will give the market the confidence that it requires to invest more and to invest better. Several OECD member and non-member countries have developed or are considering developing taxonomies of sustainable finance. Taxonomies link into the work of major international governmental platforms such as the Central Bank's Network for Greening the Financial System, or the Coalition of Finance Ministers for Climate Action, with the OECD being an observer on both platforms.

At the cross roads between environment and finance, sustainable finance taxonomies can be part of the policy toolkit for better investment for better lives. The present report proposes initial policy considerations in relation to definitions of sustainable finance. The OECD stands ready to assist governments and international dialogue in their taxonomy related work.

Rodolfo Lacy, Director, Environment Directorate.

# Acknowledgements

This report was produced by the OECD Environment Directorate, directed by Rodolfo Lacy, and the Climate, Biodiversity and Water Division led by Simon Buckle. This report was written by Mireille Martini, under the supervision of Robert Youngman who provided careful review and guidance, inputs, and encouragement. The authors are grateful to Simon Buckle for his involvement in and support to the role of OECD as an observer to the EU Technical Expert Group on Sustainable Finance, which laid the ground for this report. They also express thanks to Nassera Belkhiter, Inès Reale, Sama Al Taher Cucci, Beth Del Bourgo, Jane Kynaston, Elvira Berrueta-Imaz, Pascale Denoyer and the support teams of the Division. The authors are responsible for any errors or omissions. This report has benefited from discussions with the following OECD experts: Brilé Anderson, Geraldine Ang, Barbara Bijelic, Timothy Bishop, Gérard Bonnis, Chloé Desjonquères, Lisa Danielson, Alexander Dobrinevski, Catherine Gamper, Raphael Jachnik, Katia Karousakis, Takayoshi Kato, Kumi Kitamori, Kate Kooka, Xavier Leflaive, Jean-François Lengelle, Michael Mullan, Daniel Nachtigall, Edward Perry, Andrew Prag, Mikaela Rambali, Dirk Röttgers, Tsuzuri Sakamaki, Cecilia Tam, Aayush Tandon. The authors are grateful for the valuable advice, time and inputs received from external experts who were consulted at various points and to various degrees during the preparation of this work, and would like to thank in particular Sean Kidney (Climate Bonds Initiative) and Emmnanuel Buttin and Guido Moaveri-Milanesi (European Commission). This work benefitted significantly from the generous support of the Japanese government.

# Table of contents

## Tables

# Reader's guide

This report is composed of two parts. Part 1 contains the essence and analytical content of the report. It provides a summary presentation of the sustainable finance definitions and taxonomies in the five jurisdictions involved (EU, China, Japan, France and the Netherlands). It proposes a mapping of theses definitions and taxonomies, and preliminary reflections on policy considerations. Part 2 of the report is descriptive. It provides a detailed review of sustainable finance definitions and taxonomies in the jurisdictions in the scope of the report. Chapter 7 contains an overview of EU taxonomy regulation, and a summary of the technical screening criteria for eligibility that were proposed by the EU Technical Expert Group to the European Commission in June 2020.

# Abbreviations and acronyms

| | |
|---|---|
| **CBI** | Climate Bonds Initiative |
| **CITE** | Crédit d'Impôt Transition Energétique (Tax rebate for energy efficiency improvements) |
| **DNSH** | Do No Significant Harm |
| **ESG** | Environmental, Social and Governance |
| **EU TEG** | European Union Technical Expert Group on Sustainable Finance |
| **GBP** | Green Bonds Principles |
| **GRI** | Global Reporting Initiative |
| **ICMA** | International Capital Markets Association |
| **ILO** | International Labour Organisation |
| **IPSF** | International Platform on Sustainable Finance |
| **KPI** | Key Performance Indicators |
| **MDB** | Multilateral Development Bank |
| **MNE** | Multi National Enterprise |
| **MOEJ** | Ministry of Environment of Japan |
| **OAT** | Obligation Assimilable du Trésor |
| **PBOC** | People's Bank of China |
| **SASB** | Sustainability Accounting Standards Board |
| **SDG** | Sustainable Development Goals |
| **TCFD** | Taskforce for Climate related Financial Disclosures |

# Executive summary

## The momentum around sustainable finance taxonomies

In recent years, investors have increasingly taken actions to integrate climate change and broader sustainability concerns into their investment decisions and portfolio allocations. However, there is a widely perceived need for greater certainty on the environmental sustainability of different types of investments and economic activities. In response, a number of jurisdictions have started to legislate to create official definitions of sustainable finance. This report maps sustainable finance definitions and taxonomies in five jurisdictions: the EU, China, Japan, France and the Netherlands.

Taxonomies are definitions of sustainable finance that aim to be comprehensive classification systems, while definitions of sustainable finance are less ambitious in scope. When appropriately designed, sustainable finance definitions and taxonomies can bring potential benefits. These include improving market clarity. More precise and consistent definitions of which investments are "green" and "sustainable" could facilitate investment by giving confidence and assurance to investors. Other potential benefits include easier tracking of sustainable finance flows in order to measure them, and/or in order to to take a policy action such as setting incentives.

Recognising some of those potential benefits, the European Union (EU) adopted in June 2020 a regulation to establish a framework to facilitate sustainable investment. This regulation, often referred to as "the EU Taxonomy Regulation", is the cornerstone of the EU Sustainable Finance Action Plan, as it will feed into several forthcoming regulatory initiatives such as the EU Green Bond Standard, the EU Ecolabel for retail investment funds and others.

Several other jurisdictions also have addressed sustainable finance taxonomies and definitions. In China, the People's Bank of China issued the first iteration of its Green Bond Endorsed Project Catalogue, commonly referred to as "the Chinese taxonomy", in 2015. In Japan, the Ministry of the Environment of Japan (MOEJ) launched Japan's green bond guidelines in 2017. The Netherlands has had a legislative approach to green lending since 1995 (Green Funds Scheme), and France created the GreenFin label for retail investment funds in 2015. Other countries expressing interest on sustainable finance taxonomies include Canada, Kazakhstan and Indonesia.

## Policy makers have diverse options to design taxonomies

Taxonomies or definitions (henceforth "taxonomies") can cover a diverse range of environmental objectives, from climate mitigation to a broader set of environmental objectives (adaptation, water, circular economy, pollution, biodiversity…), and can include social and governance objectives (or not do so). Such environmental and other objectives may be independent or interdependent. For instance an activity may only qualify on one dimension if it also fulfils criteria relating to other dimensions, such as the "Do no significant harm" condition in the EU Taxonomy. Taxonomies can also have diverse "colours". For example, they may identify economic activities and/or financial products that are already compliant with environmental objectives ("green" or "dark green"). Additionally or alternatively, they may identify activities that are on a transition pathway to become green ("transition" or "light green").There may be a role for "brown taxonomies" as well, i.e. taxonomies identifying activities which are not judged compatible with environmental objectives.

An additional design consideration is the incorporation of the notion of a systems approach. Based on the OECD contribution to the EU Technical Expert Group on Sustainable Finance (TEG), the EU taxonomy recognises that an economic activity cannot be considered truly sustainable independent of the wider system in which it operates. An equally important design consideration is the need to reflect multiple pathways. There are many potential emissions pathways to a given environmental objective, and different jurisdictions will have different long-term climate policy objectives and will follow different pathways. How pathways are translated to the level of a corporate issuer is also a topic for careful consideration. Taxonomies should also be adaptable to evolving knowledge and technologies as well as the adjustment of transition pathways in view of results achieved over time.

The introduction of government-sponsored taxonomies may significantly increase demand for data from issuers and investors in order to check eligibility of activities and/or investments. The issue of data availability is central to the uptake of taxonomies. The implementation of taxonomies requires a degree of standardisation of the data provided, to allow for aggregation and assessment of compliance in a way that is consistent and comparable.

A related consideration is the likely "ease of use" of a taxonomy. This issue is particularly important at present, notably for smaller operators, when economies worldwide are already coping with economic and financial impacts and pressures created by COVID-19 response measures. Overstretched financial and human resources may be unable to implement new frameworks easily. Making taxonomy compliance achievable for smaller corporates and financial market participants could involve, for example, using a proportionality approach when designing compliance and verification criteria.

## Mapping taxonomies in five jurisdictions: commonalities, differences and gaps

Among the taxonomies and definitions examined in this report, the EU taxonomy is unique in the level of detail in taxonomy compliance requirements that it achieves. It also is the only framework that interlinks six environmental objectives together through the multi-dimensional "Do No Significant Harm" (DNSH) requirement. Keeping in mind these essential differences, commonalities can be identified for renewable energy and green buildings, where metrics and thresholds among the scoped definitions are similar. By contrast, in other sectors such as non-renewable power generation and transport, international investors will find that sectoral coverage is similar across jurisdictions but criteria for inclusion differ. Only the EU taxonomy includes certain hard-to-abate manufacturing sectors such as cement, steel, aluminium and hydrogen. Finally, some gaps in terms of sectors not covered can be identified in all frameworks, including the aviation and health sectors.

Many issuers and investors will have activities and investments across several jurisdictions. A taxonomy reflecting only a single jurisdiction and its associated activities will not allow issues and investors to cover all of their international activities or investments. To resolve this issue, the TEG has identified certain criteria in the EU taxonomy as being of "international relevance", meaning that users of the taxonomy could use them for economic activities located outside the EU. Other issues around international comparability of taxonomies are discussed in the International Platform on Sustainable Finance (IPSF), launched by the EU in 2019 to enhance international cooperation where appropriate. The OECD is an observer to the IPSF.

## Perspectives

The mapping provided in the present report establishes that there is already a basis for a common language on sustainable finance taxonomies for international issuers and investors that are willing to use such a tool. In individual jurisdictions, well-designed taxonomies can help policy makers to develop and grow sustainable finance markets to support the achievement of environmental and other sustainable development goals.

# Part I Developing sustainable finance definitions and taxonomies

# 1 Introduction

Sustainable finance definitions and taxonomies have a significant potential to mobilise investment in the context of a broader supportive policy framework. The report analyses official definitions and taxonomies of sustainable finance in five jurisdictions: the EU, Japan, China, France and the Netherlands.

## 1.1. Why sustainable finance definitions and taxonomies matter

Scaling up financial flows in support of climate and sustainability objectives is critical. According to the 2017 OECD report Investing in Climate, Investing in Growth, investment needs for infrastructure are estimated to be around USD 6.3 trillion annually between 2016 and 2030 (OECD, 2017[1])[1]. Taking into account the additional needs to reach a 2°C temperature goal, the estimate increases by 10% to USD 6.9 trillion. Yet annual investments are well below this level at USD 3.3-4.4 trillion (OECD/The World Bank/UN Environment, 2018[2]).

Policy makers need to make use of a range of policy levers to help address this investment gap, to scale-up sustainable investment and to move away from unsustainable investment. These levers, which have been examined in several other OECD reports, include, but are not limited to: domestic clean energy policy frameworks, comprising core climate policies (e.g. carbon pricing, fossil fuel subsidy reform) and broader investment conditions; development of markets for green financial products; climate risk disclosures and other actions to address supply side investment barriers; the creation and strengthening of institutions and programmes to use interventions (e.g. risk mitigation) to mobilise sustainable infrastructure investment and create markets; and project pipeline preparation in the context of (sustainable) infrastructure planning. This report focuses on another policy lever which recently has received increased attention: sustainable finance definitions and taxonomies. These definitions are being developed in response to a perceived need for greater certainty on the environmental sustainability of different types of investments and economic activities. A starting point for this report is that such definitions and taxonomies are only one part of the range of policies needed to mobilise investment, but that they have significant potential to mobilise investment in the context of a broader supportive policy framework.

In recent years, investors have to an increasing extent taken actions to integrate climate change and broader sustainability concerns into their investment decisions and portfolio allocations. Diverse financial market actors have engaged in a broad range of sustainability-related initiatives within various contexts and with diverse objectives. As a result, there are many different understandings of which investments are sustainable.

As explored in more detail in this report, the multiplicity of definitions of "green" and "sustainable" investments is often cited as an important barrier to scaling up green and sustainable investment. Previous OECD analysis on green bonds notes that, "The lack of universal rules and standardisation is a shared and enduring source of concern cited by participants in the market. Convergence towards commonly accepted definitions will be essential to maximise the effectiveness, efficiency and integrity of the market." (OECD, 2017[3]). Differences in policies and standards relating to sustainable investments can result in market fragmentation. It is increasingly recognised that such policy and market fragmentation may constrain the financing of, and investment in, transition-compatible assets, such as renewable energy infrastructure (OECD, 2016[4]).

## 1.2. Sustainable finance definitions and taxonomies considered in this report

### 1.2.1. Five jurisdictions

In view of these concerns, a number of jurisdictions have started to legislate to create official definitions of sustainable finance products. For example, the EU put forward in May 2018 a regulation on the establishment of a framework to facilitate sustainable investment. This regulation was adopted by EU co-legislators in December 2019, and published in the Official Journal of the European Union in June 2020. It is usually referred to, and will be referred to in this report, as "the EU taxonomy". A taxonomy is a scheme of classification, and is broader than a definition. In the case of the EU taxonomy, it is a framework for defining the conditions for an economic activity to be considered as environmentally sustainable as per the

EU legislation. Experts in the OECD Secretariat (Environment Directorate) have contributed to important aspects of the development of the EU taxonomy through the OECD's participation as an observer in the European Commission's Technical Expert Group on Sustainable Finance (TEG). The EU sustainable finance taxonomy was not the first sustainable finance taxonomy; in 2015, the People's Bank of China issued a Green Bond Endorsed Project Catalogue, also commonly referred to as "the Chinese taxonomy".

The analysis includes sustainable definitions from three other countries: France, the Netherlands and Japan. France has used sustainable finance definitions for several years. It created two label schemes for investment funds, the GreenFin label and the ISR (Socially Responsible Investment) label. The Dutch State also has had legislation on green loans and green funds, since 1995. These two countries have also issued sovereign green bonds, allowing for consideration of the definitions of eligible expenditure under those frameworks. Even if green bond frameworks may not constitute a legislative definition in the strict sense, the way in which a government implements sovereign green bond financing is indicative of its thinking on green finance and eligible green activities. The situation in Japan was also examined. A large actor in global financial markets outside the EU, Japan does not have a taxonomy or definitions of sustainable investments, and has not issued a sovereign green bond. However, Japan has issued a green bond framework, which is included in the mapping of definitions.

The present report focuses on these five jurisdictions for pragmatic purposes, and to allow for a detailed comparison of selected definitions and taxonomies. An increasing number of countries have developed, are developing, or have signalled interest in developing definitions and taxonomies. Subsequent work on taxonomies could aim to compare a broader set of countries. Some countries such as Canada and Kazakhstan have expressed their intention to legislate on sustainable finance definitions. In the latter case, the OECD has undertaken work on the design of a taxonomy. In addition, Indonesia, one of the countries included in OECD's Clean Energy Finance and Investment Mobilisation (CEFIM) programme, issued a sovereign green bond in 2018. Indonesia has also developed a sustainable finance roadmap, including guidelines for banks.

### *1.2.2. Official definitions and taxonomies rather than market-based practices*

The focus of this work is on legislative definitions, and as such it leaves aside all market and institution-based definitions of sustainable finance. Such excluded definitions include those used by Multilateral Development Banks, on a stand-alone basis or in association with the MDB Common Principles for Climate Mitigation Finance Tracking. The Climate Bonds Initiative (CBI)'s taxonomy is also not included, but discussed briefly in Section 1.3.2 as it plays an important role in the green bond market. This voluntary taxonomy, developed by CBI (an "international, investor-focused not-for-profit"), is applied by private issuers of green bonds seeking to receive the "Climate Bonds Certification". In addition, this analysis excludes the many taxonomies used by large financial institutions, each of them different. However, to provide further context for legislative definitions, Part 1 includes some details on market and institutions-based definitions.

## 1.3. Issues addressed in this report

In the EU and beyond, the EC legislative action stirred a debate in the financial and regulatory community on the definitions used for identifying environmentally sustainable investments. The debate revolves around three main issues. Firstly, what is the merit of legislative action, compared with letting the financial markets use their own definitions (as they have been doing for some time)? Secondly, if legislative definitions are preferred, how should they be designed? Thirdly, given the fact that financial markets are global, is there merit in (and any constraints to) international co-ordination of definitions for environmentally sustainable investments?

This report presents elements of answers on the first two issues above. It contains an overview of sustainable finance definitions and taxonomies in the five said jurisdictions (Chapter 2 of this report), and a discussion on key issues around design and implementation (Chapter 3 of this report). Part 2 of the report presents, whenever possible, the detailed principles, metrics and thresholds used in each jurisdiction to assess compliance with a sustainable finance definition or taxonomy. A comparison by sector is provided in Chapter 4, in order to identify the sectors in which different jurisdictions' approaches are similar, and the sectors where different approaches exist. This work could pave the way for future guidance on good practice for taxonomy design. Initial desk research done for this review suggests that in some cases the information on metrics and thresholds may not be readily accessible, for language or accessibility issues or both.

## References

OECD (2017), *Investing in Climate, Investing in Growth*, OECD Publishing, Paris, https://dx.doi.org/10.1787/9789264273528-en. [1]

OECD (2017), *Mobilising Bond Markets for a Low-Carbon Transition*, Green Finance and Investment, OECD Publishing, Paris, https://dx.doi.org/10.1787/9789264272323-en. [3]

OECD (2016), "Fragmentation in clean energy investment and financing", in *OECD Business and Finance Outlook 2016*, OECD Publishing, Paris, https://dx.doi.org/10.1787/9789264257573-10-en. [4]

OECD/The World Bank/UN Environment (2018), *Financing Climate Futures: Rethinking Infrastructure*, OECD Publishing, Paris, https://dx.doi.org/10.1787/9789264308114-en. [2]

## Notes

[1] The 2017 report considered a scenario with 66% probability of achieving 2 degrees Celsius (based on available economic models). It is important to highlight that the Paris Agreement aims to hold the increase in the global average temperature to well below 2°C above pre-industrial levels – which likely would require even higher levels of sustainable infrastructure investment.

# 2 Overview of sustainable finance definitions and taxonomies

This chapter provides an overview of sustainable finance taxonomies in five jurisdictions: the EU, Japan, China, France and the Netherlands. The overview provides a synopsis of the environmental objectives (e.g. climate change mitigation, adaptation) and sectors (power generation, etc...) covered by the taxonomies.

## 2.1. Overview of the emerging EU taxonomy

This section briefly describes the emerging EU taxonomy, and then analyses its key features. The main characteristics of the emerging EU taxonomy are that it addresses economic activities, located in the European Union, on a mandatory basis, with a multi-criterion framework, including transition activities, with stringent thresholds and with no verification framework identified yet.

### 2.1.1. Brief description

On June 20, 2020, the "Regulation on the establishment of a framework to facilitate sustainable investment" was published at the Official Journal of the European Union (EUOFFICIALJOURNAL, 2020[1]). This regulation sets a framework for the taxonomy design. The details for implementing the regulation, called Technical Screening Criteria, will be developed progressively over time. The regulation will enter into force in stages between 2021 and 2022.

The EC Action Plan on Financing Sustainable Growth (European Commission, 2018[2]), published in March 2018, includes ten initiatives (including the taxonomy), and has three stated objectives:

- Reorient capital flows towards sustainable investment, in order to achieve sustainable and inclusive growth
- Manage financial risks stemming from climate change, environmental degradation and social issues
- Foster transparency and long-termism in financial and economic activity.

The EU taxonomy aims at defining which economic activities can be considered as sustainable as per European legislation. The definition of sustainability includes social elements on top of environmental objectives. The six environmental objectives identified for the purposes of the taxonomy are:

1. Climate change mitigation
2. Climate change adaptation
3. Sustainable use and protection of water and marine resources
4. Transition to a circular economy
5. Pollution prevention and control
6. Protection and restoration of biodiversity and ecosystems.

For an economic activity to be considered taxonomy-compliant, it must:

1. Contribute substantially to one or more of the environmental objectives
2. Do No Significant Harm to any other environmental objective
3. Comply with minimum social safeguards (the OECD Guidelines for Multinational Enterprises and the UN Guiding Principles on Business and Human Rights, including the International Labour Organisation's ('ILO') declaration on Fundamental Rights and Principles at Work, the eight ILO core conventions and the International Bill of Human Rights).

The Technical Expert Group on Sustainable Finance (TEG) developed principles, metrics and thresholds for substantial contribution to climate change adaptation and mitigation (including Do No Significant Harm screening criteria) for 72 economic activities. Those economic activities belong to the following economic sectors: agriculture, forestry, manufacturing, electricity, waste, water, transport, buildings, and Information and Communication Technologies. The TEG issued an interim report in June 2019 on which a public consultation was held from July to September (EUTEG, 2019[3]). The TEG produced its final reports in March 2020 (EUTEG, 2020[4]) (TEG, 2020[5]). The EC will use these final reports as a basis to produce the Delegated Acts to implement the taxonomy regulation.

Economic activities, even when making a substantial contribution to climate change mitigation, will not be eligible if they cannot be performed in a way that avoids significant harm to other environmental objectives. Substantial contribution (as per 1 above) and Do No Significant Harm (as per 2 above) are assessed on the basis of general principles, metrics and thresholds.

An example of principles is technology neutrality: the selected criteria must not discriminate amongst technologies, provided they have the same impact on environmental objectives. An example of a metric is grams CO2e/kWh for power generation, with a Life Cycle Assessment required or not, depending on activities (EUTEG, 2019, p. 236[3]). Thresholds (e.g. 100 gr CO2e/kWh for power generation) were identified on the basis of existing EU legislation when available. Otherwise, they were assessed based on current technological performance, taking into account foreseeable technological developments, in consultation with some 150 external experts plus internal EC experts.

For example, passenger cars must not only meet climate mitigation objectives (a), but also must not significantly harm other environmental objectives, including pollution (b). For (a), the TEG proposed a threshold of tailpipe intensity of 50 gr CO2/km until 2025, and 0 gr CO2/km after 2025. For (b), the TEG proposed compliance with the emission thresholds for clean light-duty vehicles in Table 2 in the Annex of Directive (EU) 2019/1161 of the European Parliament and of the Council of 20 June 2019 amending Directive 2009/33/EC on the promotion of clean and energy-efficient road transport vehicles (EUTEG, 2020, pp. 339,341[4])

### *2.1.2. Addressing economic activities, not financial products*

The regulation defines environmental sustainability criteria for economic activities, not for financial products. Further legislative guidance will be provided on how to use the regulation for financial products. The EC is preparing an Ecolabel regulation that will define sustainability criteria for investment funds.

With definitions applying to economic activities, the existing taxonomy regulation is not readily usable for firms. For instance, the regulation defines conditions under which the economic activity "construction of a water project" can be considered as a sustainable activity. One can infer that the shares or the debt of a company solely involved in this activity will therefore be considered as a sustainable investment. However, this activity could be undertaken by a construction and civil works company that is also involved in building highways and/or airports, which are not among the economic activities eligible for sustainable tagging by the EU regulation. Therefore, it will be necessary to have a rule allowing for calculation of this civil works company's overall sustainability (and of its shares or debt) based on its full range of economic activities. Such a rule could consider, for example, the percentage of its total sales or investments attributable to sustainable activities.

In a similar vein, a rule will be necessary for determining whether a financial product is taxonomy-compliant. An example of financial product is an investment fund. It may hold a variety of assets, including debt and equity securities of firms. A rule such as the percentage of taxonomy-compliant holdings over the total holdings of the fund[1] will be necessary to assess the taxonomy-compliance of the whole investment fund.

### *2.1.3. Mandatory regulation*

The EU taxonomy is a mandatory scheme in the sense that financial market participants will be obliged to comply with the regulation when they want to market a financial product as "environmentally sustainable as per EU legislation". It is worth noting that an issuer, for instance a bank, will still be able to issue a (self-labelled) "transition bond" with no reference to the EU taxonomy, as long as the bank does not mention "environmentally sustainable" in communications on the transition bond. This feature is consistent with the legislators' intention, which is not to impose prescriptions on financial markets, but rather to spur the development of a market for "environmentally sustainable" investments as defined in the regulation. The achievement by the EU taxonomy of this objective will depend on whether financial market participants will adopt the EU taxonomy in lieu of other alternatives, including their existing in-house classification frameworks.

### *2.1.4. A multi-criterion framework*

The regulation defines six environmental objectives. In order to be eligible, an economic activity must be checked at the same time against the six objectives, one for "substantial contribution" and the five others for "Do No Significant Harm". Therefore, all environmental objectives are interlinked together in the EU taxonomy framework. This feature is significant and unique. None of the other four definitions considered in this analysis interlinks various objectives in this way, or seeks to do so. In practice, however, this approach may raise usability issues. Demonstrating such multi-criteria compliance could involve significant time and costs from financial market participants and/or corporates.

### *2.1.5. Applicable to activities located within the European Union*

More than 80% of the "Do No Significant Harm" (DNSH) criteria identified so far[2] refer to existing EU environmental regulation. So, if other jurisdictions were to apply the EU taxonomy, they would need to apply also the corresponding part of EU environmental regulation. Furthermore, the 72 activities currently considered in the EU taxonomy have been selected based on the highest emitting sectors and the highest emissions reduction potential[3]. Other jurisdictions may wish to prioritise other activities.

Financial institutions such as asset managers hold global investment portfolios, notably with holdings in the US and Japan, but also Switzerland and "off-shore financial centres"[4]. For these global institutions, it may be useful to have a taxonomy of sustainable finance that may cover holdings in various jurisdictions beyond the EU. There is an emerging dialogue initiated by the EC on an international approach to sustainable finance definitions (see section below).

### *2.1.6. Transition and enabling activities included in addition to low-carbon activities*

An important area of debate around the EU taxonomy has related to its scope. Some were expecting the EU taxonomy to be "pure green" – i.e. to limit eligible activities to those associated with a near-zero or zero-carbon economy. At the other end of the spectrum, others wanted the taxonomy to include "all colours". Such a framework would provide a comprehensive screening system that would enable the ranking of a whole portfolio from "pure green" to "dark brown", and any activities that might be characterised by other colours (e.g. those with ambiguous or no climate implications, such as the health or media sectors).

In light of the above, the following considerations may be of interest:

- The EU taxonomy is first of its kind in aiming to address multiple environmental goals as well as social and governance objectives.
- Integrating these multiple considerations in a taxonomy can provide a means for policymakers to ensure that sustainable finance supports the achievement of not only the Paris Agreement, but also other environment-focused Sustainable Development Goals (SDGs) as well as social objectives in the SDGs.
- Having multiple criteria will add complexity and costs to reporting, but there are already many precedents for taking ESG criteria into account both within the scope of this study (e.g. green bonds) and outside the scope (e.g. Multilateral Development Banks (MDBs) investment guidelines).
- The EU taxonomy's approach (Contribute substantially to one or more of the environmental objectives, Do No Significant Harm to any other environmental objective) is one of potentially many approaches that could be taken. It differs, for example, from other impact measurement

approaches. Some of those impact measurement approaches in principle could help steer finance to projects with the greatest impact. However, they likely would involve higher costs than the EC approach, which (for mitigation) involves assessment against a threshold rather than measurement of impact. There is already concern among some potential taxonomy users that the EC taxonomy's approach will be too burdensome and costly due to data gaps. In addition, it remains to be seen whether a single agreed approach for impact measurement for all relevant ESG considerations can be achieved.

- Costs, data gaps and other issues are some of the disadvantages of the EC's approach to a complete taxonomy. Benefits include the ability to provide a complete picture of a portfolio of activities or investments – this will encourage firms and investors to take actions that will increase the share of their portfolio that can be described as EU sustainable. If it is used by a large share of the market, the EC approach to a complete taxonomy will make greenwashing more difficult, as users will have their sustainability share highlighted, and non-users will be questioned as to why they opted not to use the EC standard.
- In the same vein, whether there is a need for a social taxonomy could be an issue for further consideration. The EU Taxonomy addressed the social dimension by including a set of minimum social safeguards in the requirements for compliance: the OECD Guidelines for Multinational Enterprises and the UN Guiding Principles on Business and Human Rights, including the International Labour Organisation's ('ILO') declaration on Fundamental Rights and Principles at Work, the eight ILO core conventions and the International Bill of Human Rights. The lessons learnt from the first steps at implementing the EU Taxonomy will determine whether this minimum safeguards approach is needs to be complemented with further elements on a social taxonomy.

The emerging EU taxonomy includes not just low-carbon economic activities, but also two other categories: "transition" and "enabling" activities.

"Transition activities" are activities that contribute to a transition to a net-zero emissions economy in 2050, but are not currently close to a net-zero carbon emissions level. In order to be taxonomy compliant, transition activities must show that they can significantly enhance their performance beyond the industry average, without lock-in to carbon intensive assets or processes. Thresholds for compliance will tend toward zero over time, consistent with the future net-zero emissions economy[5]. One example is passenger cars, with a threshold of emissions at 50g CO2e/km until 2025, and then zero.

Enabling activities are those enabling improvement of environment performance to a fairly demanding level in other sectors of the economy. They are evaluated on a sector-by-sector basis. Examples in the current TEG report include manufacture, sale and installation, rather than operation or purchase of, highly efficient boilers and micro-renewables. Another example would be the manufacture of wind turbine blades.

### *2.1.7. Stringent thresholds*

In some cases, threshold levels are derived from trajectories to achieve net carbon neutrality by 2050 at sector level. In other examples, they derive from the requirement to match the best performers' level[6] in a given sector. Several market observers have considered the thresholds proposed by the TEG as rather stringent. The choice of stringency in thresholds is a key element in the design of a sustainable finance taxonomy. Looser thresholds favour an uptake of the taxonomy by issuers of green financial products, for whom it will be easier to find taxonomy compliant projects. Thresholds that are more stringent tend to favour an uptake by investors, who will be more confident the thresholds will ensure avoidance of green washing concerns.

Current research suggests that only a modest share of investments in infrastructure and equipment may be compliant with the current draft EU taxonomy. To examine the climate consistency of real economy investments and underlying financing, the Research Collaborative for Tracking Finance for Climate Action is completing pilot studies for individual sectors in individual countries, such as manufacturing industries in Norway (Dobrinevski, 2019[6]). One element of this work consists of an estimation of the shares of investments in infrastructure and equipment which are compliant with the criteria from the current draft of the EU taxonomy. The estimated shares for manufacturing industries in Norway that are compliant with the current version of the EU taxonomy is well below 5%.

## 2.2. Overview of taxonomies and sustainable finance definitions in other jurisdictions

This report examines definitions and taxonomies in five jurisdictions: the EU, China, France, the Netherlands and Japan. The world "taxonomy" is used only with reference to the EU and China classification frameworks. For the three other jurisdictions, sustainable finance definitions are not called taxonomies. Only sustainable definitions included in legislation or issued by government bodies were examined, as opposed to definitions based on market practice or individual institutions. The five jurisdictions have issued official definitions for green loans and green bonds (with the exception of Japan where there is no official green loan definition). The Sovereign Green Bond frameworks of France and the Netherlands were also included in the study. A summary is provided in the table below.

Table 2.1. Sources of sustainable finance taxonomies and definitions

| | China Taxonomy | EU Taxonomy | France Definitions | Netherlands Definitions | Japan Definitions |
|---|---|---|---|---|---|
| **Sources** | | | | | |
| Sovereign Green Bond | | | x | x | |
| Green loans definition in legislation | x | x | x | x | |
| Green bonds definition in legislation | x | x | x | x | x |

Source: Authors

### 2.2.1. China

Through regulations, China has created separate definitions of green credit and green bonds. What is usually referred to as the "Chinese taxonomy" is the regulation concerning green bonds.

#### *Green credit*

The China Banking and Insurance Regulatory Commission issued green lending guidelines in 2012, Green Credit Statistics Forms in 2013, and Key Performance Indicators (KPIs) for implementing the guidelines in 2014. There are no environmental criteria or thresholds mentioned in the English translation of these documents. Further research would be necessary of identify environmental criteria and metrics if they exist. Banks are required to report every six months the loan balance of credits identified as green, and report the impacts of these credits on energy savings and emissions reductions, as well as water savings. Green credit sectors are agriculture and forestry, energy and water saving, nature protection, ecological restoration and disaster prevention projects, waste disposal, recycling and pollution prevention, clean energy, rural clean water projects, green buildings and green transportation. Green loans meeting eligibility requirements and having at least a double-A (AA) credit rating can obtain preferred central bank refinancing.

### Green bonds

Under the supervision of the People's Bank of China (PBOC), a China Green Bond Endorsed Project catalogue was issued in 2015 (Green Finance Committee, 2015[7]). The catalogue applies to green bonds issued by financial institutions. Green bonds may be used as collateral for low-interest central bank loans, which gives financial institutions an incentive to issue them. The six categories of eligible green bonds are energy savings, pollution prevention and control, resource conservation and recycling, clean transportation, clean energy and ecological prevention and climate change adaptation. The catalogue provides detailed criteria and thresholds, in the form of references to domestic industrial standards and regulations. The PBOC also issued guidelines for listed and non-listed domestic corporate bond issuances, which are aligned with this taxonomy. Large banks such as Bank of China, Industry and Construction Bank of China, and the Development Bank of China, have tapped global markets with green bonds, using international standards (more specifically, the Climate Bonds Standard issued by CBI).

As noted by CBI, "In 2018, green bond issuance from Chinese issuers aligned with international practice for green bond issuance reached 31.2 billion US dollars. Internationally aligned green bonds from Chinese issuers account for 18% of global issuance, with China the largest country of issuance after the United States. If bonds that align only with China's local definitions are factored in, total issuance in 2018 reached 42.8 billion US dollars." (CBI China Green Bond Market, 2019[8])

## *2.2.2. Japan*

The Ministry of Environment of Japan (MOEJ) issued Green Bond Guidelines in 2017 (MOEJ, 2017[9]), and a guide for good adaptation practice by the private sector. The Guidelines aim at promoting issuance of domestic green bonds while ensuring the reliability of the environmental benefits of green bonds and reducing the costs and administrative burdens of issuers. The Guidelines are consistent with the widely recognised International Capital Market Association's Green Bond Principles. Under the Japanese Green Bond Guidelines, funds procured through green bonds must be allocated to green projects that have clear environmental improvement effects. Issuers should evaluate and disclose these effects, and quantify them to the maximum extent possible. Metrics are provided in the following sectors: renewable energy, energy conservation, pollution prevention and management, sustainable management of natural resources and land use, biodiversity conservation, clean transportation, sustainable water resource management, adaptation to climate change, environmentally friendly manufacturing technologies and processes, and green buildings. The MOEJ supports green bond issuance by subsidising issuers' costs of establishing a green bond framework and of securing an external review.

## *2.2.3. France*

### Green investment funds: the GreenFin and ISR Labels

French legislation has defined "green investments" within the context of the GreenFin label (formerly named Transition Energétique et Ecologique, or "TEEC") (Ministere de la Transition Ecologique, 2019[10])for investment funds. The label is based on the Climate Bonds Initiative (CBI) taxonomy (see below) for green bonds. It defines three categories of issuers of financial securities: those with more than 50% of their sales coming from an activity identified as "green" by CBI; those with between 10 and 50% of sales from a green activity; and those with between 0 and 10% of their sales in green activities. For each category of investment funds, levels are set for the maximum permissible percentage of "minimally green" issuers' securities and the minimum permissible percentage of "very green" issuers' securities, measured as a percentage of the Net Asset Value of the investment fund. For private equity funds, the threshold is 75% of the Net Asset Value (NAV) of the fund in securities from issuers with at least 50% of their sales compliant with the CBI taxonomy. The label has been in existence since 2015 and is managed by the Ministry for the Ecological Transition (MTE). The label has been awarded to 40 investment funds to date, with net assets under management of 11.5 billion euros. France also has an Environment, Social and Governance (ESG) label (Label ISR, Investissement Socialement Responsable). The label targets investment funds with good ESG practices and verification. This label, which is less stringent than the GreenFin label, has received more uptake, with 210 labelled funds accounting for 54 billion euros under management.

*France's Sovereign Green Bond: the Green OAT (Obligation Assimilable du Trésor)*

The French state raised a total of 20.5 billion euros under its sovereign green bond (Green OAT, Obligation Assimilable du Trésor) (Agence France Trésor, 2018[11]) in several tranches. Eligible expenditures under the Green OAT framework (Agence France Trésor, 2017[12])are some central government budget expenditures, and expenditures under the Invest for the Future programme (Programme pour les Investissements d'Avenir, PIA). Proceeds are managed like those of a conventional sovereign bond, but allocations of expenditures to the Green OAT are tracked and reported. More than 50% of allocations need to relate to current or future years' expenditures; other allocations can relate to past years' expenditures. Expenditure should relate to one of the six following green sectors: building, transport, energy (including smart grids), living resources, adaptation, pollution control and eco-efficiency. Nuclear energy, armament and all expenditure dedicated to fossil fuels are excluded. The four environmental objectives addressed are climate change mitigation, adaptation, biodiversity and pollution.

The 2018 allocation went for 60% to mitigation objectives, 20% to adaptation objectives, 13% to biodiversity and 7% to pollution relevant objectives. In terms of sectors, 38% of the 2018 allocation went to the buildings sector, 15% to living resources, 13% to transport, 7% to energy, 15% to adaptation and 11% to multisector destinations. Examples of expenditures are studies and research, together with investments in sustainable forestry or the maintenance of French waterways under an investment programme to increase waterborne transport. Buildings expenditures are mainly the refinancing of a tax rebate to homeowners on energy efficiency improvements (CITE, Crédit d'Impôt pour la Transition Energétique). The OECD sits on the evaluation committee for the Green OAT.

### 2.2.4. The Netherlands

The Netherlands has not developed a sustainable finance taxonomy per se. However, the Dutch government offers a wide range of green financial support instruments mostly in the form of targeted grants and tax reliefs. It also put in place a specific legislation and financial incentive scheme for green mortgages. In May 2019 the Netherlands became the first AAA sovereign to issue a green bond.

*The green funds scheme*

The Netherlands has had since 1995 a detailed legislative approach to green lending, with a high degree of involvement of the retail banking sector. The Green Funds Scheme (RVO, 2010[13]) incentivises retail and corporate lending for housing, agriculture and nature such as individual greenhouses in farms, transport, public works and water management. The Scheme is coordinated between four Ministries: Housing and Spatial Planning, Agriculture, Public Works/Water Management and Finance. The scheme includes environmental criteria and thresholds and comes with lower costs of funding for banks enabling lower lending rates for clients.

*The green mortgage scheme*

The Netherlands also issued legislation in 2016 to create a green mortgage scheme, in which homeowners or buyers provide energy savings certificates for purchase or renovation works. The certificate enables them to borrow on cheaper terms. By linking energy efficiency investments to mortgages, the programme aims to facilitate and greatly expand such investments.

A study reported in a Dutch National Bank position paper in 2017, "Bottlenecks in funding of green investment", found that based on data from 1997 – 2017, out of the 45% of homeowners who invested in making their home more energy efficient[7], only 4% financed this investment by borrowing. The study was based on a sample of 1588 home owners-occupiers. Of the households not making investment to green their homes in the past ten years, a mere 1.4% said this was due to their not being able to get a bank loan. More frequently stated reasons include a lack of savings and aversion to run up debt. High installation costs, and difficulty to compare costs and benefits, were also quoted. This suggests that the green mortgage scheme may not have had a significant direct impact on accelerating investment in "greening homes".

*The Sovereign Green Bond*

The Netherlands issued a sovereign green bond in 2019 with part of the allocation destined to fund the Delta Programme for sustainable water management and resilience to increased sea levels. Eligible expenditures are limited to central government budget expenditures in the budget year preceding the issuance, the budget year of the issuance and future budget years. Sectors covered are renewable energy, climate change adaptation and sustainable water management, clean transportation (passenger railway and linkage of cycling to other modes of transportation), energy efficiency of residential homes.

The following sub-chapters will situate these official definitions within the broader universe of definitions used by market practitioners in the five jurisdictions, including those not issued by government bodies.

## 2.3. Other institutional and market-based definitions of sustainable finance

In the five jurisdictions considered for this study, other institutional and market-based definitions of environmentally sustainable finance are in use. The following brief, non-exhaustive review of such definitions is intended to shed light on the broader context in which legal definitions or taxonomies operate.

### *2.3.1. Institutional definitions*

The OECD tracks climate finance provided and mobilised by developed countries (OECD, 2019[14]). In addition, the OECD is working on methodologies for tracking investment consistent with achieving a low greenhouse gas development (Jachnik, Mirabile and Dobrinevski, 2019[15]).

Multilateral Development Banks (MDBs) have issued since 2015 joint Common Principles for Climate Mitigation Finance Tracking and (separately) for Adaptation Finance Tracking. This is a joint effort by International Development Finance Club (IDFC), the World Bank Group, the African Development Bank (AfDB), the Asian Development Bank (ADB), the European Bank for Reconstruction and Development (EBRD), and the European Investment Bank (EIB). Each of those banks and the members of IDFC also use their in-house definitions to track and publish the amount of climate and/or sustainable finance they handle (see for instance EIB's yearly sustainability report (EIB, 2019[16])). Definitions vary among these MDBs, and were not scoped in detail for the purpose of the present research.

### *2.3.2. Widely used market-based definitions*

The most widely used framework is the private, market-based Climate Bonds Initiative (CBI) standard (the Climate Bonds Standard). CBI issues a detailed, sector- based taxonomy (CBI, 2020[17]) to complement its standard. The Climate Bonds Initiative is a non-profit organisation involved in certifying green bonds worldwide. In 2019, the amount of green bonds issuance aligned with CBI definitions amounted to 231 billion US dollars, and the amount of labelled green bond issuance aligned with CBI definitions amounted to 189 billion US dollars (CBI, 2020[18]).

The CBI taxonomy broadly covers the same economic activities as the EU taxonomy. However, the EU taxonomy differs from the CBI taxonomy because of its design: for a given economic activity, the EU taxonomy uses a matrix approach, where six sets of metrics and thresholds are used, one for each environmental objective. In contrast, the CBI taxonomy uses only one metric/threshold, and is focused on climate mitigation, rather than other environmental objectives. As stated in the CBI taxonomy, « it identifies the assets and projects needed to deliver a low carbon economy and gives GHG emissions screening criteria consistent with the 2-degree global warming target set by the COP 21 Paris Agreement » (Climate Bonds Initiative, 2020[19]).

Another framework is the voluntary Green Bonds Principles (GBP) framework, issued by the market association International Capital Markets Association (ICMA). Issued in 2014 and updated in 2016, the GBP provided a framework for the process of issuing a green bond. The procedural standardisation provided by this framework, which is fully incorporated into the Climate Bonds Standard, appears to have supported the rapid growth of the green bond market. However, stakeholders using the GBP framework have noted that different standards for assessing greenness (Climate Bond Standard, shades of green, others) and verification (second party opinion, third party assurance, etc.) create concerns about inconsistencies and the potential for greenwashing. Further information on the GBP framework is provided in the OECD report "Mobilising Green Bonds for the Low Carbon Transition" (OECD, 2017[20]).

In this context, the EU TEG was tasked with developing recommendations for the European Commission regarding a future legislation on an EU Green Bond Standard. The TEG recommended that the EC propose a standard in 2020, "aligned with the EU taxonomy", but not necessarily exactly matching the requirements, given the fact that the taxonomy is not likely to be fully implementable before 2022. The TEG also recommended that second opinion verifiers be systematically accredited through an ad hoc EU supervisory body.

### *2.3.3. Non-financial reporting frameworks*

Other relevant classification and assessment schemes for investments and economic activities include non-financial reporting frameworks like the Sustainability Accounting Standards Board (SASB) and the GRI (the Global Reporting Initiative).

The Sustainability Accounting Standards Board, SASB, is one of the most widely used frameworks. This independent non-profit organization was set up with the support of the Bloomberg group in 2012. It has 25 000 mostly corporate users in 200 countries (50% in the US, 25% in Europe). It provides Environmental, Social and Governance (ESG) information, with a financial materiality angle, i.e. which ESG considerations can materially impact financial performance. It developed 77 industry specific disclosure standards with metrics, which feed into communications to investors in addition to financial accounting.

Another widely used framework, complementary to SASB, is the GRI. The Global Reporting Initiative (known as GRI) is an international independent standards organization that helps businesses, governments and other organizations understand and communicate their impacts on issues such as climate change, human rights and corruption. Although the GRI is independent, it remains a collaborating centre of UNEP and works in cooperation with the United Nations Global Compact. It is mainly used as a basis of corporate extra financial reporting for corporate social responsibility (CSR) or environmental, social and governance (ESG) report. First launched in 2000, GRI's sustainability reporting framework is now widely used: in 2017, 63 percent of the largest 100 companies (N100), and 75 percent of the Global Fortune 250 (G250) reported applying the GRI reporting framework. The most recent of GRI's reporting frameworks are the GRI Standards, launched in October 2016. As far as climate change disclosure frameworks are concerned, the leading instrument seems to be the Financial Stability Board's Task Force on Climate-related Financial Disclosures (TCFD). The EC guidelines on reporting climate related information, published in June 2019 (European Commission, 2019[21]), supplement the existing 2017 guidelines to the NFRD and integrate the recommendations of the TCFD[8].

### 2.3.4. In house taxonomies

Most large financial institutions are using their own standards and definitions to count and report their "climate finance", or Paris-aligned or transition-aligned finance. One of the issues for uptake of the voluntary EU taxonomy is how far the final taxonomy will be from non-financial reporting standards that financial institutions currently use, like GRI, and therefore what will be the time and costs involved to adapt to the new EU standard.

The preceding overview of non-legislative standards defining climate and/or sustainable finance is not exhaustive. There is a proliferation of standards. In addition to standards that have been used in various developed markets, separate standards are under consideration in a number of emerging economies.

## 2.4. Countries considering taxonomy development, and the International Platform for Sustainable Finance (IPSF) of the EU

### 2.4.1. Canada

In June 2019, the Expert Group on Sustainable Finance appointed by the Canadian government - and perhaps inspired by the EU High Level Expert Group on Sustainable Finance (convened at the end of 2016) - delivered its final report. One of the Expert Panel's recommendations was for the Government of Canada to work with the private sector to develop a green and transition-oriented fixed income taxonomies. The Canadian Standards Association (CSA Group) has convened a committee, comprised of private sector experts, to develop a taxonomy of activities that would qualify for "green" or "transition" financing in Canada through dedicated instruments like green or transition bonds and loans.

### 2.4.2. Kazakhstan

As of 2019, Kazakhstan is working with the OECD Secretariat (Environment Directorate) in implementing the project "Introduction of Green Growth Indicators and Preparation of the Report on Green Growth in Kazakhstan". The main objective of the project is to assist Kazakhstan in integrating the measurement of green growth into the regulatory reporting system, in implementing the concept for the transition to a green economy, in assessing progress and achieving green growth. As part of this work, insights from the EU TEG experience and the EU taxonomy were shared with relevant interlocutors in the country.

### 2.4.3. Indonesia

The OECD Secretariat (Environment Directorate) is working with the Indonesia government under the Clean Energy Finance and Investment Mobilisation programme (CEFIM, 2019[22]). Indonesia's Financial Services Authority (thereafter, OJK) launched the country's first Sustainable Finance Roadmap in 2015. OJK defined standards in 2017 for green bond issuance. Furthermore, Bank Indonesia (the country's central bank) became a member of the Network for Greening the Financial System (NGFS) in 2019. Indonesia's Ministry of Finance (MoF) issued the country's first sovereign green sharia-compliant bond (or green sukuk) in 2018 with proceeds allocated to sustainable transportation (46%) and climate resilience (40%), with the remainder used for energy efficiency (10%) and renewable energy (4%) (MinistryofFinance, 2019[23]).

### 2.4.4. The EU IPSF

At the Climate Action Summit in New York in September 2019, the EU launched an International Platform on Sustainable Finance (Commission, 2019[24]). Members of the Platform are the EU and national, non-EU governments. The aim of the Platform is to exchange and disseminate best practices in environmentally sustainable finance, to compare the different initiatives and identify barriers and opportunities to help scale up environmentally sustainable finance internationally. The Platform also aims at enhancing international cooperation where appropriate, while respecting national and international contexts. To date, members of the IPSF are the EU and Argentina, Canada, Chile, China, India, Kenya and Morocco. Observers are the Coalition of Ministers for Climate Action, the EBRD, the EIB, and the International Organisation for Securities Commissions, the Network for Greening the Financial System, the UNEP-FI and the OECD. The IPSF held its first Sherpa meeting back-to-back with the OECD Forum on Green Finance and Investment on November 30, 2019 at the OECD, and is currently mapping sustainable finance definitions among its members.

## 2.5. Table: Overview of sustainable finance definitions and taxonomies

The table below summarizes the landscape of sustainable finance taxonomies and definitions addressed in this report. A cross in a box indicates that there is an official text in the country addressing the issue.

## Table 2.2. Sources, incentives, objectives and sectors in sustainable finance definitions and taxonomies

| | China Taxonomy | EU Taxonomy | France Definitions | Netherlands Definitions | Japan Definitions |
|---|---|---|---|---|---|
| **Sources** | | | | | |
| Sovereign Green Bond | | | x | x | |
| Green loans definitions in legislation | x | x | x | x | |
| Green bonds definitions in legislation | x | x | x | x | x |
| Incentives | | | | | |
| Interest rate incentives | x | | x | x | |
| Tax incentives or subsidies | x | | x | x | x |
| Monetary policy/collateral incentives | x | | | | |
| Objectives | | | | | |
| Social objectives included | x | x | x | | |
| Climate change adaptation | | x | x | x | x |
| Climate change mitigation | x | x | x | x | x |
| Water and marine protection | x | x | x | x | x |
| Pollution prevention and control | x | x | x | x | x |
| Waste and recycling | x | x | x | x | x |
| Ecosystems/Biodiversity | x | x | x | x | x |
| Sectors covered | | | | | |
| Nuclear | | ? | | | |
| Gas with emissions threshold | | x | | | |
| Clean fuel | x | | | | |
| Clean Coal (supercritical) | x | | | | |
| Hydro | x | x | x | x | x |
| Solar | x | x | x | x | x |
| Wind | x | x | x | x | x |
| Biofuels (biogas, biomass) | x | x | | x | |
| Power Transmission and distribution | x | x | x | x | |
| Energy efficiency | x | x | x | x | x |
| Green buildings/energy efficiency in buildings | x | x | x | x | x |
| Private passenger transport | x | x | x | x | |
| Public passenger transport | x | x | x | x | |
| Freight rail | x | x | x | x | |
| Waterborne transport | x | x | x | | |
| Water infrastructure | x | x | x | x | |
| Clean water supply | x | x | x | | |
| Forestry | x | x | x | x | x |
| Fisheries and aquaculture | | x | x | | x |
| Preparation, re use, recycling | x | x | x | x | |
| Waste to energy | x | x | x | x | |
| Clean steel | | x | | | |
| Clean aluminium | | x | | | |
| Clean cement | | x | | | |
| Low carbon technologies | | x | | | |
| Hydrogen | | x | | | |
| Information and Communication Technology | | x | | | |

Source: Authors

Building on the above overview of legal and market-based definitions of sustainable finance used in the five jurisdictions considered in this report, Chapter 3 of the report addresses a number of issues regarding their design and the purpose they are supposed to serve.

## References


Agence France Trésor (2018), *https://www.aft.gouv.fr/files/medias-aft/3_Dette/3.2_OATMLT/3.2.2_OATVerte/Green%20allocation%20and%20performance%20report%202018.pdf*. [11]

Agence France Trésor (2017), *https://aft.gouv.fr/files/archives/attachments/25562.pdf*. [12]

CBI (2020), *https://www.climatebonds.net/*. [18]

CBI (2020), *https://www.climatebonds.net/standard/taxonomy*. [17]

CBI China Green Bond Market (2019), *https://www.climatebonds.net/files/reports/china-sotm_cbi_ccdc_final_en260219.pdf*. [8]

CEFIM (2019), *https://www.oecd.org/cgfi/resources/OECD-clean-energy-finance-and-investment-mobilisation-programme.pdf*. [22]

Climate Bonds Initiative (2020), *https://www.climatebonds.net/files/files/CBI_Taxonomy_Tables_January_20.pdf*. [19]

Commission, E. (2019), *Press release: The European Union and countries worldwide join their forces to mobilise private investors for financing the green transition*, https://ec.europa.eu/info/files/191018-international-platform-sustainable-finance-press-release_fr. [24]

DNB (2017), *https://www.dnb.nl/en/news/news-and-archive/dnbulletin-2017/index.jsp*. [26]

Dobrinevski, A. (2019), *Working Party on Climate, Investment and Development Exploring options to measure the climate consistency of real economy investments The manufacturing industries in Norway*. [6]

EIB (2019), *https://www.eib.org/en/publications/sustainability-report-2019*. [16]

EUOFFICIALJOURNAL (2020), *https://eur-lex.europa.eu/legal-content/EN/TXT/PDF/?uri=CELEX:32020R0852&from=EN*. [1]

European Commission (2019), *https://ec.europa.eu/finance/docs/policy/190618-climate-related-information-reporting-guidelines_en.pdf*. [21]

European Commission (2018), *EC Action Plan on Financing Sustainable Growth*, https://eur-lex.europa.eu/legal-content/EN/TXT/PDF/?uri=CELEX:52018DC0097&from=EN. [2]

EuropeanCommission (2018), *EC Regulation on the establishment of a framework to facilitate sustainable investment*, https://eur-lex.europa.eu/legal-content/EN/TXT/PDF/?uri=CELEX:52018PC0353&from=EN. [25]

EUTEG (2020), *https://ec.europa.eu/info/sites/info/files/business_economy_euro/banking_and_finance/documents/200309-sustainable-finance-teg-final-report-taxonomy-annexes_en.pdf*. [4]

EUTEG (2019), *EU TEG Taxonomy Technical Report*, https://ec.europa.eu/info/sites/info/files/business_economy_euro/banking_and_finance/documents/190618-sustainable-finance-teg-report-taxonomy_en.pdf. [3]

Green Finance Committee (2015), *http://greenfinance.org.cn/displaynews.php?cid=79&id=468*. [7]

Jachnik, R., M. Mirabile and A. Dobrinevski (2019), "Tracking finance flows towards assessing their consistency with climate objectives", *OECD Environment Working Papers*, No. 146, OECD Publishing, Paris, https://dx.doi.org/10.1787/82cc3a4c-en. [15]

Ministere de la Transition Ecologique (2019), *https://www.ecologie.gouv.fr/sites/default/files/Label_TEEC_labellisation_r%C3%A9f%C3%A9rentiel_0.pdf*. [10]

MinistryofFinance, I. (2019), *Green sukuk Allocation and Impact report*, https://www.sdgphilanthropy.org/system/files/2019-02/Green%20Suku%20Issuance%20-%20Allocation%20and%20Impact%20Report%20.pdf. [23]

MOEJ (2017), *http://www.env.go.jp/en/policy/economy/gb/gl_point_en.pdf*. [9]

OECD (2019), *Climate Finance Provided and Mobilised by Developed Countries in 2013-17*, OECD Publishing, Paris, https://dx.doi.org/10.1787/39faf4a7-en. [14]

OECD (2017), *Mobilising Bond Markets for a Low-Carbon Transition*, Green Finance and Investment, OECD Publishing, Paris, https://dx.doi.org/10.1787/9789264272323-en. [20]

RVO (2010), *https://www.rvo.nl/sites/default/files/bijlagen/SEN040%20DOW%20A4%20Greenfunds_tcm24-119449.pdf*. [13]

TEG, E. (2020), *https://ec.europa.eu/info/sites/info/files/business_economy_euro/banking_and_finance/documents/200309-sustainable-finance-teg-final-report-taxonomy_en.pdf*. [5]

Zoromé (2007), *https://www.imf.org/external/pubs/ft/wp/2007/wp0787.pdf*. [27]

## Notes

[1] Such a rule would also need to establish the methodology for this measurement (book value or net asset value for instance).

[2] The Technical Expert Group had only one year to deliver, as a recommendation for EC legislation, indicative thresholds and screening criteria to effectively implement its multi-criterion approach. Given the complexity of the task and the tight timeframe, it was not possible for the TEG to deliver "do no significant harm" criteria across all geographies of the EU. Work is continuing to provide the remaining DNSH criteria.

[3] As well as some other secondary considerations such as supplementing the NACE code framework if appropriate for instance in order to add a "buildings" sector, whilst "buildings" do not correspond to a NACE code.

[4] An Offshore Financial Centre is defined as a country or jurisdiction that provides financial services to non-residents on a scale that is incommensurate with the size and the financing of its domestic economy (Zoromé, 2007[27]). They include Jersey, Guernsey, Isle of Man, Singapore and Hong-Kong, among others.

[5] Remembering this is perhaps an economy-wide goal and that not all sectors will be able to reach net zero even later in the century.

[6] For example using the EU ETS benchmark, see below.

[7] Via insulation or sustainable energy.

[8] The final TCFD recommendations contain the following statement : "The Task Force considered existing voluntary and mandatory climate-related reporting frameworks in developing its recommendations and provides information in the Annex on the alignment of existing frameworks, including those developed by the CDP (formerly the Carbon Disclosure Project), Climate Disclosure Standards Board (CDSB), the Global Reporting Initiative (GRI), the International Integrated Reporting Council (IIRC), and the Sustainability Accounting Standards Board (SASB), with the Task Force's recommended disclosures."

# 3 Key issues for sustainable finance definitions and taxonomies

For most countries, taxonomies are a tool that policymakers can use to spur sustainable investment and improve market clarity and integrity. Their potential users include corporates, financial institutions and retail investors. Key design considerations for sustainable finance taxonomies include integrating pathways to environmental objectives, and a taking a systems approach with respect to designating eligible economic activities. Key usability issues include data availability.

## 3.1. The role of taxonomies in the sustainable finance landscape

### *3.1.1. Taxonomies as a toolkit*

This chapter focuses on sustainable finance definitions and taxonomies as systems of classification for sustainable economic activities and/or financial products. There are two dimensions to a taxonomy: the system itself in all its complexity, and the final product (boiled down to its pragmatic essentials) as it will be used by financial market participants and other users (see below for a discussion on usability issues). Users of taxonomies and definitions are not necessarily interested in understanding why a given metric or threshold must be used for an activity. Rather, they will use the taxonomies and definitions as a final product and screen activities to determine eligibility under the taxonomy. By contrast, policy makers can design the classification systems in various ways. For them, taxonomies are toolkits. By organising the classification system in a number of ways, they can pursue a number of environmental and broader sustainability policy objectives. Sustainable finance taxonomies can be tools to articulate sustainability policy objectives, and are a potentially important element of sustainability policies. A possible analogy could be a smartphone. Smartphone users are not concerned with the internal design and operation of the product. They use the system for a range of practical purposes. Analogously, financial market participants using taxonomies would be smart phone users, and policy makers would be smart phone designers, devising the system to enable and produce a set of functionalities.

### *3.1.2. Who can use taxonomies and how*

The expected user response is a key driver of the design of a system. The issue of who are the users of sustainable finance definitions and taxonomies, and what these users can expect from the definitions and taxonomies, is therefore relevant. Different users have different goals and opportunities.

#### *Policy makers*

The stated goal of many sustainable finance definitions is to attract capital to sustainable investment. For instance, the initial proposal for the EU taxonomy regulation states that "[setting out] uniform criteria for determining whether an economic activity is environmentally sustainable… would help ensuring that investment strategies are oriented towards economic activities which are genuinely contributing to the achievement of environmental objectives" (EuropeanCommission, 2018, p. 2[11]). This could be done in many ways – e.g. by signalling what is sustainable, providing incentives for what is considered sustainable etc. A possible measure for the success of definitions could therefore be the amount of additional capital that they attract to sustainable investment, compared to a situation where no official definition existed.

Taxonomies and definitions may be more effective in attracting capital when accompanied by incentives. In turn, the development of incentives relies on taxonomies, as financial products need to be defined before being incentivized. The budgetary cost of providing incentives needs to be considered against the benefits of attracting capital to sustainable investment. In addition, pricing externalities such as carbon emissions may be more economically efficient than providing incentives tied to investments that have varying environmental and social impacts. However, different incentive measures can complement each other, e.g. carbon pricing to make emission-reducing projects and assets more economically attractive, and incentives to promote issuance of and investment in financial products linked to a taxonomy. In addition, financial product-based incentives can be particularly important when pricing for externalities is too low to significantly drive investment.

#### *Corporates*

For taxonomies and definitions to be used, corporates will have to provide the data that is necessary to assess compliance with the threshold included in a taxonomy. One example is the reporting of carbon emissions. Providing data is an opportunity for corporates to improve their performance in addressing climate and sustainability issues and incorporating them in their strategies. A recent survey in the U.K. (Harvey Nash, n.d.[2]) indicates that 46% of boards of publicly listed companies spent zero hours discussing climate change in 2019. However, when the use of definitions is voluntary, there is the danger that those corporates that are already engaged in the low-carbon transition could be burdened with additional reporting if they want to claim the eligibility of their financing, while those not engaged would escape the costs and constraints.

*Financial markets institutions: asset owners, asset managers and banks*

Sustainable finance definitions are an opportunity for asset owners, asset managers and banks to signal the alignment of their existing and future portfolios. For many institutions, sustainable finance is a new frontier, with both a commercial (attracting investment) and reputational aspect. Transparency in terms of data and methodologies will help avoid the danger of green washing[1]. For financial market participants, like for corporates, those applying a demanding legislative but voluntary taxonomy may come at a disadvantage to those keeping their in-house methodology at no adaptation cost.

*Retail investors*

A potential use of taxonomies and definitions is to make sustainable finance more accessible to retail investors. Because of the regulation protecting retail savings in many countries, precise definitions of what is "green" or sustainable may be necessary to market this customer base. This is important not just as a potential channel of additional retail capital to match sustainable investment needs. Retail investors are also citizens and voters, and the definitions and selling channels of sustainable finance products can be an opportunity for retail investor engagement in the policy dialogue.

## 3.2. Important considerations to incorporate into taxonomies

The design of classification systems may be a primary determinant of where sustainable investments will flow moving forward. For example, the EU sustainable finance taxonomy is described as providing "...practical guidance for policy makers, industry and investors on how best to support and invest in economic activities that contribute to achieving a climate neutral economy." (EuropeanCommission, 2019[3]). Even when the use of a taxonomy is not mandatory and when there are no associated incentive measures, a taxonomy can be expected to spur investment in specific areas and deter investment in other areas. The assumption is that issuers of financial products will use the taxonomy in response to and anticipation of demand from investors, who will be motivated to make their portfolios, or a portion of their portfolios, more consistent with the taxonomy, in view of reputational, risk- or opportunity-related considerations. The use of incentive measures to promote the use of the taxonomy, or even the potential that incentives will be provided in the future, would strengthen the impact of a taxonomy in accelerating and steering investment.

The question of what activities should be eligible for the "sustainable" designation (or other designations, such as "transition") raises many issues for policy-makers and market actors. For example, in the (relatively narrow) context of climate mitigation policy, the types and level of private sector investments that the government assumes will be made in response to current and planned policies may be estimated in economic models and therefore "known" in a hypothetical sense. However, by setting eligibility thresholds in taxonomies, governments are making these assumptions much more concrete and applicable to investors. Within the bounds and applicability (voluntary or mandatory) of any given taxonomy, the government is no longer leaving to the market the question of what types of investments the market will make in response to or in anticipation of climate policies. Therefore, decisions on thresholds and other eligibility considerations may be seen as having both immediate and long-lasting consequences for investment.

In order to meet climate mitigation objectives, governments will need to consider carefully a range of factors to help ensure that taxonomies drive the “right” types of low-carbon investments. Given the multitude of pathways (see section 3.2.1 below) to meet long-term climate objectives, and the political economy implications of enabling some but not other types of investments, governments will have differing views on which activities should qualify, and how to define eligibility. These different views can be expected to lead to differences among taxonomies. In addition, other considerations, such as approaches for assessing sustainability beyond climate mitigation, could tend to increase differences among taxonomies. Nevertheless, some common approaches for taxonomies could be considered to limit differences in a way that facilitates international investment without unnecessarily constraining national decision-making on how the low-carbon, sustainable transition will be undertaken.

Another important consideration in designing taxonomies relates to usability; users must find that a taxonomy is usable and practical to be effective in influencing investment. Usability may be subjective and difficult to assess. Furthermore, policy-makers may reasonably expect users to go through a period of learning by doing and to endure some level of transaction costs in adapting to the taxonomy and addressing knowledge and data gaps and other challenges. At the same time, policy-makers need to keep practicability firmly in mind to ensure that taxonomies can meet their intended goal – steering and accelerating investment in selected areas. For example, as discussed in the previous chapter, the green mortgage scheme in the Netherlands may not have had a significant direct impact on accelerating investment in “greening homes”, because only a tiny portion of those home owners occupiers doing green investment in their homes actually finance the investment with a bank loan.

The following discussion provides a non-comprehensive overview of important considerations for taxonomies. Building on this discussion and dialogues with experts and governments, technical guidance could be developed to help inform sustainable finance taxonomy design efforts.

### *3.2.1. Integrating pathways and a systems approach*

#### *Integrating pathways in the design of taxonomies*

Some of the voluntary definitions in use in financial markets focus on screening an economic activity or investment based on a metric that is applied today. For instance, geothermal electricity generation facilities are eligible in the Climate Bonds Initiative taxonomy when their direct emissions are less than 100 gr CO2e per kWh. By contrast, the EU taxonomy is screening a number of activities on the basis not just of a threshold met today, but also of a future trajectory that the activity must follow. This has been a significant input from OECD to the work of the TEG. In the case of geothermal electricity generation, the EU taxonomy reads: “Facilities operating at life cycle emissions lower than 100 g CO2e/kWh, declining to 0 g CO2e/kWh by 2050, are eligible”. Other jurisdictions have different long-term climate policy objectives and will follow different pathways, which could be reflected in their sustainable finance definitions and taxonomies Integrating a future intended trajectory in the criteria embeds a pathway for emissions in the taxonomy. In the case of the EU, the specific pathway is explicit, as the taxonomy refers to a policy objective of reaching carbon neutrality by 2050. Integrating pathways into definitions and taxonomies can help avoid lock-in of emitting activities and assets, and to help ensure that eligible investments will be compatible with long-term policy objectives.

However, pathways have a number of complexities and raise several issues. One is that there are many potential (global) emissions pathways to a given goal, so choosing one of them for the taxonomy requires careful consideration of implications (just as such a choice would require careful thought for other aspects of sustainability policies). For instance, a “net zero carbon economy” in 2050 is not an economy where all economic activities are zero emitting, but an economy where unavoidable remaining emissions are compensated with negative emissions activities. Thus, taxonomies aiming for a net zero carbon economy will need to incorporate thresholds such that some sectoral activities phase out emissions completely by 2050 while others reflect best available technologies and expectations (updated regularly) on the future evolution of BAT. The IPCC SR 15 report in October 2018 (Allen et al., 2018[4]) outlined the many pathways that are compatible with climate objectives.

A second issue worth considering here is that different countries will have different transition pathways. For instance, the trajectories to a net zero economy by 2050 is likely to involve quite different sectors and thresholds in India and in Germany, while both these countries' net zero trajectories would contribute to a global net zero by 2050 scenario.

A third issue is that if a pathway can be identified for a given economic activity, an approach is still needed to translate the pathway or pathways to the level of a corporate. Corporates rarely operate with only one activity. This means that in order to assess the degree of alignment of a corporate with a given pathway, it is necessary to have defined pathways for several activities, with a methodology to aggregate them at corporate level, consistent with a global pathway calculation. For instance, a civil works company will carry out work and possibly own assets in diverse sectors such as water, electricity generation, transport, etc. Multinational enterprises bring additional complexity, as they operate in various countries. They need to consider pathways not only in different sectors but also in various countries. The exercise can become quite complex and even impossible to carry out, for methodological and/or data availability reasons.

In practice, most definitions, when they use a pathway (which can vary significantly by country) refer to a straight declining line. For example, the EC and CBI use a pathway to zero carbon in 2050 and refers to a straight declining line for the sectors' emissions (although sectors have different targets, as noted above). Country and sector pathways will however be very different depending on starting conditions, so that this apparent convergence and simplicity may disguise the complexities noted in the preceding discussion. Even if several countries aim to put themselves on such a pathway, and incorporate the pathway in their national taxonomies, there are still a range of considerations and assumptions in translating the pathway to the taxonomy that may lead to (perhaps inevitable) differences in corporate-level thresholds among different taxonomies.

### *Integrating a systems approach in the design of taxonomies*

Based on the OECD contribution to the TEG, the EU taxonomy incorporates the notion of a systems approach to economic activities. As stated on page 42 of the EU TEG interim report (EUTEG, 2019[5]) "An economic activity cannot truly be considered sustainable independently from the wider system in which it operates. For example, the emissions reductions enabled by an electric vehicle depend a number of factors: charging from low-carbon electricity sources, not adding to congested traffic conditions and whether, at the end-of-life stage, the battery is reused or recycled in an environmentally sustainable way. Similarly, the well-being of people in cities does not just depend on the availability of low-emissions residential housing for example, but necessitates access to low-emissions transport options to ensure access to places of work and other vital services (shops, health facilities, etc.) or urban planning that lessens the need for vehicles . [.....] The taxonomy development approach has therefore aimed to identify activities that make a substantial contribution on their own but also enable the overall transition of critical systems such as the energy, transport, urban, water and food systems. However, the nature of the transition in each country or region is influenced by the evolution of the entire system, including local strategies and policies. A taxonomy-eligible activity may only contribute to an individual country or region's transition pathway when it is also coherent with the transition of the overall system of which the activity is a part."

The EU taxonomy therefore acknowledges the usefulness of a systems approach. Awareness of systems issues by market actors and policymakers, for example, can and should lead to innovation, new thinking on eligibility criteria for certain activities, and updated criteria. In practice, the concept has been partially operationalised notably in the setting of Do No Significant Harm criteria for certain activities. For example, the DNSH criterion for the manufacture of hydrogen reads: "The main potential significant harm to other environmental objectives from the manufacture of hydrogen is, in practical terms, inseparable from the potential for significant harm created by the hydrocarbon refining activity more generally. It is associated with polluting emissions to air; water used for cooling might lead to local resource depletion, dependent of the local scarcity of water resources; and the generation of wastes." (EUTEG, 2020, p. 181[6]).

Further operationalising efforts of a systems approach may need to consider how to provide further and more granular guidance to taxonomy users who are non-experts in systems approaches, and likely will have varying interpretations. Other taxonomies and definitions reviewed in this report do not appear to incorporate a systems approach, even at the high level reflected in the EC taxonomy.

### *3.2.2. Adapting to innovation and technology development*

A desirable feature of a sustainable finance taxonomy is that it does not lag behind market innovation, or changes in available knowledge. A taxonomy should be able to adapt to the appearance of new technologies and to the start of the art of climate and environmental science. Consequently, a challenge of designing a taxonomy is the need to ensure sufficiently frequent updates to minimise any lag behind market innovation. As important new innovations and technology developments emerge, it will be important that the taxonomy will be responsive and evolve accordingly.

It can be argued that the absence of a mandatory or government-endorsed taxonomy enables innovation in the market. Unencumbered by taxonomies, which in practice cannot be updated constantly, new projects can push the boundaries of our current understanding of best practices in green buildings, for example. On the other hand, in a market without a government-endorsed taxonomy or other broadly recognised standard, innovations may remain relatively hidden to many market participants, given the myriad of different voluntary eligibility criteria being applied by different actors in the market. Moreover, such innovations could come with a trade-off; a proliferation of voluntary criteria also enables relatively weak thresholds (and green washing) to remain relatively hidden.

To help ensure the EU taxonomy is an adaptable framework, the TEG intermediary report (EUTEG, 2019[5]) states: "The taxonomy thresholds must be updated, with the phasing out of some included activities until specific points in time, as well as adaptation to the latest technological developments and innovation." (p 186). The legislation includes a three-year revision clause for the activities and thresholds included. In addition, the EC intends to set up a platform where corporates and financial market participants will be able to advise on innovation requiring update of the activities and thresholds.

Setting ambitious thresholds in a taxonomy framework can itself spur innovation, by inciting corporates to better their environmental performance to match the threshold. For example, the EU taxonomy uses the EU-Emissions Trading System's (EU-ETS) direct emissions benchmarks as a threshold for determining substantial contribution for mitigation in the primary aluminium production sector. The EU-ETS benchmark corresponds to the average emissions of the 10% most greenhouse gas efficient installations in a given sector included in the EU-ETS system. As of June 2019, the value of the threshold is 1.514 $CO_2e$/t. The EU taxonomy threshold will automatically adjust in line with adjustments in the benchmark.

### *3.2.3. Linking taxonomies design with sustainability policies*

In ongoing work on the theme of "climate change mitigation through a well-being lens", the OECD is considering interactions between climate mitigation and other policy objectives. "Adopting a well-being lens means ensuring that decisions aim to deliver simultaneously on multiple well-being objectives, including climate. It also requires an economy-wide perspective, rather than focusing on a single or very narrow range of output-related objectives, independently of others. For example, tackling damaging air pollution problems by eliminating fossil-fuel combustion takes advantage of one of the major synergies between climate action and health. In terms of trade-offs, addressing in advance the potential impacts on the affordability of transport from increased fuel prices through targeted compensatory measures or investments in public transport infrastructure, makes such price increases more acceptable and effective". (OECD, 2019, p. 2[7])

Because taxonomies can integrate a systems approach, and more generally can be designed in a number of ways, they can also take into account broader well-being objectives. These include environmental as well as social issues. Depending on policy-makers' priorities for sustainable finance, taxonomies have the potential to embrace a multiplicity of dimensions. For example, by interlinking six environmental objectives with the substantial contribution/do no significant harm approach, the EU taxonomy achieves a multiple dimension approach in its design. As outlined in section 1.1.1 above, the EU taxonomy includes a social dimension in sustainability. It requires eligible activities to comply with minimum social safeguards (the OECD Guidelines for Multinational Enterprises and the UN Guiding Principles on Business and Human Rights, including the International Labour Organisation's ('ILO') declaration on Fundamental Rights and Principles at Work, the eight ILO core conventions and the International Bill of Human Rights).

In sum, sustainable finance classification systems can embed in their design a pathways and systems approach, and integrate multiple objectives to pursue different inter-related dimensions of sustainability. The EU taxonomy is a pioneering effort to implement an integrated approach. Other definitions considered in this report currently focus on a single objective.

## 3.3. Usability issues in taxonomies

The introduction of government-sponsored sustainable finance definitions and taxonomies may significantly increase demand for data from issuers and investors in order to check eligibility of activities and/or investments.

### *3.3.1. Data availability*

The taxonomies and definitions reviewed in this report require users to provide or obtain data to prove compliance with the required metrics. In some cases, e.g. for green bonds, the data needs to be provided by issuers. In other cases, like the French GreenFin label, the data is to be provided by asset managers, who can obtain it from corporates but also get it from data providers, who provide their own calculations based on data and metrics provided by corporates.

In the case of the draft EU taxonomy, the level of data required from issuers or corporates is still to be detailed in the forthcoming delegated acts accompanying the taxonomy legislation. Most of the DNSH criteria for mitigation are requirements in existing EU environmental law. Many issuers, particularly smaller ones, are therefore said to be complying "by default" with this extensive range of legislation; however, this assumes a meaningful level of compliance assessment and enforcement, which often may not be the case. In addition, issuers may not have the data infrastructure in place to demonstrate compliance if necessary. It is therefore likely that data will be missing. In an initial user test case developed inside the TEG, about one third of companies in the sample portfolio could not be assessed because the necessary data was not available.

The issue of data availability is central to the uptake of taxonomies and sustainable finance definitions. In the same way that there are many different definitions of green finance, there is also a variety of methodologies for reporting certain metrics, such as carbon emissions. It is not only the scope (1, 2 or 3) of emissions that varies across reporting schemes, but also the consolidation scope within a group of companies. Some groups use the same scope as for International Financial Reporting Standards (IFRS) or US Generally Accepted Accounting Principles (GAAP) accounting to compute emissions at group level, while others use an ad-hoc perimeter. There are also various standards for counting emissions over time in the life cycle of a project. Because of this, it is difficult for investors to compare between reported emissions, or to add up corporate emissions at a portfolio level. For instance, the French securities market regulator Autorité des Marchés Financiers (AMF) issued a report in November 2019 on the social, societal and environmental disclosures of corporates listed in France (AMF, 2019[8]). It found that "While a good level of comparability between companies in the same sector is to be expected, key performance indicators are generally difficult to compare from one company to another. This is because the methodologies used and the choices made in the use of these methodologies (emission factor, calculation method, etc.) differ. Similarly, indicators are not always accompanied by sufficient explanations to allow the quality and scope of the information to be assessed." Thus, even when data is available, it may be that it cannot be aggregated between the different economic activities of a given company, or between the different companies in the portfolio of an investment fund.

Further developments in the EU taxonomy are likely to require data on environmental objectives such as pollution, water and biodiversity protection and waste and recycling. Given that this data is not generally available to corporates now, there are questions as to whether they will make the effort to provide the data or simply opt to use a voluntary market-based taxonomy framework instead. It may be that European regulators will push for more corporate disclosures in the future, notably via revisions to the Non-Financial Reporting Directive expected in 2020. It remains to be seen at which pace an ecosystem of environmental sustainability data, consistent, comparable and that can be aggregated, will develop, and what will be the respective roles of corporates and data providers in this development.

### *3.3.2. Data verification*

The inclusion of metrics and thresholds for taxonomy eligibility in legislation points to the need for verification of the statements of compliance made by financial market participants and/or corporates. For private labels, such as the Climate Bond Standard and Certification Scheme (Climate Bonds Initiative), a system of verification by private consultants, called second opinion providers, has been developed. In the EU, the TEG recommended the future creation of an EU Green Bond Standard, and the creation of a platform of second opinion verifiers that would need to receive an accreditation from the EC. As regards the EU taxonomy, the process for verification is not addressed in the current legislation, so questions remain regarding this aspect of implementation. In other schemes such as the Dutch green bonds scheme, public authorities are responsible for verifying the green credentials submitted by borrowers and given by banks.

One of the stated objectives of official definitions of sustainable finance, for example in the EU and Japan, is to limit the risk of green- or impact washing, i.e. the misleading claim that a given investment has environmental and/or social benefits. The existence of official standards and definitions will not guarantee against greenwashing in itself, because financial market participants or corporates could report compliance inaccurately. This could result from intentional wrongdoing, for instance to claim the benefits of incentives on sustainable finance products. This could also result from unintentional mistakes, particularly at a time when indicators are still new and not familiar to their users. Therefore, the quality of the verification process of a taxonomy will be particularly important to reduce the risk of green- and impact washing, and thereby to provide confidence that will enable market growth.

## 3.4. Potential benefits of sustainable finance definitions and taxonomies

Some of the potential benefits of well-designed sustainable finance definitions and taxonomies are mentioned below. In certain jurisdictions where definitions or taxonomies exist, it is perhaps possible to measure some of those benefits with appropriate indicators. This has not been attempted within the scope of the present research, but could be examined as part of future work.

### 3.4.1. Improving market clarity

More precise and consistent definitions of which investments are "green" and "sustainable" could facilitate the mobilisation and reallocation of financial capital towards those green and sustainable investments. It could give confidence and assurance to investors that they know what they are investing in, and know that their investments will be recognised as green or sustainable. Increased market clarity can in turn result in cost savings, by reducing due diligence costs. Once widely known, a green finance definition could reduce the time and effort involved in understanding and evaluating a greenness assessment methodology. More clarity may also help ease the flow of capital towards sustainability objectives. On the issuer side, greater clarity in definitions could provide greater assurance that investors will invest in the product and not hesitate due to questions about the acceptability of the definition reflected in the product. Price discovery may also be easier, as products using the same definition should be more comparable. On the investor side, definitions could make the tagging of investment products easier, and therefore increase the likelihood that an investor will express an appetite for a green investment.

### 3.4.2. Improving market integrity

*Avoiding green washing*

The fear of "green" or "impact washing" may be hindering the mobilisation of capital towards green and sustainable assets. Common standards and issuing principles are essential for growing bond markets and preventing "greenwashing" scandals that would damage the reputation of bond issuers and investors alike (Inderst, Kaminker and Stewart, 2012[9]) (Kaminker et al., 2013[10]) (OECD, 2015, p. 47[7]). The strength of a taxonomy's verification processes are therefore crucial to avoiding the risk of green and impact washing. Concerning the EU Taxonomy, the regulation does not contain details of the verification procedures, which may be clarified in the future. As far as green bonds are concerned, external review and certification costs seem to have come down over time, as the market was growing. A similar evolution for sustainable finance taxonomies would be desirable.

*Avoiding a "sustainable bubble"*

A general aim of sustainable finance definitions is to attract capital to investment objectives. Sustainable investment opportunities will depend on their risk-return profile, which is affected by such considerations as the current state of regulation and policies, such as carbon pricing. The availability of finance at the right cost plays a role, but may not suffice to shift capital towards a sustainable economy if other sustainability policies are not implemented. In this context, there could be a danger that the development of sustainable finance products creates a demand for sustainable assets, while the supply of such assets stalls due to insufficiently ambitious policies. In such a situation, increased demand for a non-increasing quantity of assets could create a price bubble. In turn, the inflation of sustainable asset prices could increase the cost of acquiring green assets for financial market participants or corporates wanting to increase their share of sustainable assets, and thereby increase the cost of the transition to a more sustainable economy.

In order to reduce such risks, policy-makers could consider how potential market growth in response to taxonomy development would match up against emerging supply of sustainability projects and assets, and aim to develop stronger targets, policies and implementation in parallel with the development and implementation of taxonomies. Taxonomies have the potential to be a powerful toolkit but they are complementary to, and not a substitute for, the need for strategic planning, good policies and regulations.

## References

Allen, M. et al. (2018), *Drafting Authors: Summary for Policymakers SPM*, https://www.ipcc.ch/site/assets/uploads/sites/2/2019/05/SR15_SPM_version_report_LR.pdf. [4]

AMF (2019), *REPORT ON THE SOCIAL, SOCIETAL AND ENVIRONMENTAL RESPONSIBILITY OF LISTED COMPANIES amf-france.org*, https://www.amf-france.org/en_US/Publications/Rapports-etudes-et-analyses/Gouvernement-d-entreprise?docId=workspace%3A%2F%2FSpacesStore%2F61824ca2-b735-455c-b23d-6132d5ce4fed. [8]

EuropeanCommission (2019), *Sustainable finance: Commission publishes guidelines to improve how firms report climate-related information and welcomes three new important reports on climate finance by leading experts*, https://ec.europa.eu/commission/presscorner/detail/en/IP_19_3034. [3]

EuropeanCommission (2018), *EC Regulation on the establishment of a framework to facilitate sustainable investment*, https://eur-lex.europa.eu/legal-content/EN/TXT/PDF/?uri=CELEX:52018PC0353&from=EN. [1]

EUTEG (2020), *https://ec.europa.eu/info/sites/info/files/business_economy_euro/banking_and_finance/documents/200309-sustainable-finance-teg-final-report-taxonomy-annexes_en.pdf.* [6]

EUTEG (2019), *EU TEG Taxonomy Technical Report*, https://ec.europa.eu/info/sites/info/files/business_economy_euro/banking_and_finance/documents/190618-sustainable-finance-teg-report-taxonomy_en.pdf. [5]

Harvey Nash (n.d.), *UK Boards Ignore Climate Change*, 2019, https://www.harveynash.com/group/mediacentre/2019/12/uk_boards_ignore_climate_change/index.asp. [2]

Inderst, G., C. Kaminker and F. Stewart (2012), "Defining and Measuring Green Investments: Implications for Institutional Investors' Asset Allocations", *OECD Working Papers on Finance, Insurance and Private Pensions*, No. 24, OECD Publishing, Paris, https://dx.doi.org/10.1787/5k9312twnn44-en. [9]

Kaminker, C. et al. (2013), "Institutional Investors and Green Infrastructure Investments: Selected Case Studies", *OECD Working Papers on Finance, Insurance and Private Pensions*, No. 35, OECD Publishing, Paris, https://dx.doi.org/10.1787/5k3xr8k6jb0n-en. [10]

OECD (2019), *In Brief Increasing incentives for climate action using a well-being lens*, https://doi.org/10.1787/2f4c8c9a-en. [7]

## Notes

[1] Further discussion of issues regarding data availability and verification is provided in section 3.3 below.

# 4 Mapping of sustainable finance definitions and taxonomies

This chapter maps sustainable finance definitions and taxonomies in the EU, Japan, China, France and the Netherlands. It identifies similarities in taxonomy design in certain sectors (forestry, renewable power generation and green buildings), as well as differences in some sectors (such as non-renewable power generation, transport and manufacturing). Other sectors (such as aviation and health) are not included in any of the taxonomies reviewed.

## 4.1. General remarks

This chapter compares and maps sustainable finance definitions in the five jurisdictions in scope. The comparison identifies similarities (section 4.2), differences (section 4.3), and gaps, i.e. areas of sustainable finance that are not covered by existing frameworks (section 4.4). The purpose of the comparison is to provide a synthesis to inform policy makers and financial market actors about the degree of comparability amongst the definitions in scope. The comparison may be helpful to investors that operate in international capital markets. It may also usefully inform other jurisdictions wishing to develop sustainable finance definitions or taxonomies by raising their awareness about what approaches already exist. The comparison is based on an analysis of each jurisdiction's definitions and taxonomies, which are presented in detail in Part 2 of the report. For brevity, the mapping in this chapter only provides summary features of definitions. The mapping is presented by sector, as most definitions are based on a sectoral approach.

A number of caveats should be kept in mind with respect to the comparison of existing definitions. EU taxonomy requirements are generally more developed than criteria in other frameworks because of the level of detail that the EC requested from the TEG in its recommendations for technical screening criteria. The EU taxonomy is the only definition that, in addition to setting criteria and thresholds for the main environmental performance area being targeted and considered (e.g. climate mitigation), also requires consideration of five other environmental performance areas. This consideration is mandated through multi-dimensional the "Do No Significant Harm" (DNSH) requirement. Other jurisdictions' definitions and frameworks also consider multiple environmental objectives, such as climate mitigation and adaptation. However, they do not include any requirement comparable to DNSH, and are in this sense uni-dimensional. They only set criteria for the main environmental performance area under consideration, and do not require that criteria relating to other environmental performance areas be met simultaneously.

Some official definitions refer to the private, market-based Climate Bonds Initiative taxonomy. This is the case for the French GreenFin label for investment funds, and for the Dutch sovereign green bond. Thus, the CBI taxonomy has on occasion been included as a reference point in the mapping, even though it does not fall within the scope of the definitions considered in this report (i.e. definitions established in national legislation). Finally, one should keep in mind that the present comparison is based exclusively on the information identified for each set of definitions, which is provided in detail in Part 2 of the report. This information derives from sustainable finance definitions set out in law. English-language official versions were used, as well as an on-line translation tool from Dutch language to English in the case of the Dutch legislation. All principles, metrics and thresholds referenced in this material were taken into account. However, metrics and thresholds not included in this material are not reflected in the report. For instance, the metrics and thresholds for green buildings renovation in China exist at various levels of local legislation (province or city), but are not available in English as far as could be investigated. In this respect, the mapping presented below represents a best-effort approach to a topic that could be revisited. Such investigation would require appropriate capabilities, e.g. language capabilities and resources in order to access and process additional material.

## 4.2. Similarities

### *4.2.1. Similarities between the EC and China taxonomies as outlined by the International Platform on Sustainable Finance*

In May 2020, the International Platform on Sustainable Finance (IPSF) set up by the EC carried out a mapping exercise for sustainable finance definitions and taxonomies, based on a survey questionnaire. The results will be presented in a report in October 2020. The survey covered the EC and China, which are included in the present report, as well as India and Canada, which are outside the scope of this report. The mapping exercise outlined a number of similarities between the EC and China taxonomies. For example, both taxonomies are mandatory. In terms of scope of application, both taxonomies address financial products, including green bonds and green loans. The overarching objectives and goals pursued are broadly similar, with the Chinese taxonomy oriented towards environmental improvement and efficient resource utilization, and the EC taxonomy having six interlinked environmental objectives. Both are binary in the sense that taxonomy compliance is a yes or no, and "different shades of green or brown" are not relevant. Both deal with economic activities and projects within selected sectors. A detailed examination of sector-level similarities is provided below.

### *4.2.2. Detailed similarities at sector level*

This section focuses on the three sectors that were found to be present in all five jurisdictions. They are: forestry, renewable energy (hydroelectricity, solar and wind power generation), and green building construction and renovation. The specifications of each framework is mapped below for these sectors. While there are differences between jurisdictions, there is a degree of convergence between approaches and metrics for those sectors. Pending closer examination of local standards in certain jurisdictions, the approaches can be deemed to be relatively comparable among jurisdictions.

#### *Forestry*

Forestry is included in all sustainable finance definitions. The criterion for forestry refers in most cases to sustainable forest management. In the EU, "Sustainable Forest Management" bears a specific meaning as it refers to a specific EU common policy framework (European Commission, 2020[11]). The CBI and Japanese criteria refer to commonly accepted international practices in Sustainable Forest Management, which include the most common certification schemes[1]. Therefore, among the different definitions, forestry criteria are not strictly identical, but are similar.

Table 4.1. Forestry criteria among definitions

| Forestry | CBI Taxonomy | EU Taxonomy | China Definitions | Japan Definitions | France Definitions | Netherlands Definitions |
|---|---|---|---|---|---|---|
| Included(yes/no) | Yes | Yes | Yes | Yes | Yes | Yes |
| Criterion | Sustainable | Sustainable | Green | Sustainable | Sustainable | Protected |
| | Forest | Forest | Forestry | Forest | Forest | Forests |
| | Management | Management | | Management | Management | |

#### *Hydropower generation*

With the exception of China, all jurisdictions include hydropower in their definitions, with a reference to the CBI taxonomy threshold of 100g CO2 e /kWh. In addition to this threshold, the EU taxonomy applies stringent "do no significant harm" conditions to hydropower, while CBI also considers environmental risks, albeit with less precise requirements. China does not have an emission threshold and signals larger projects (above 50 MW) as being eligible for green finance, with no indications of conditions relating to environmental impacts.

Table 4.2. Hydropower criteria across jurisdictions

| Hydropower | CBI Taxonomy | EU Taxonomy | China Definitions | Japan Definitions | France Definitions | Netherlands Definitions |
|---|---|---|---|---|---|---|
| Included(yes/no) | Yes | Yes | Yes | Yes | Yes | Yes |
| Criterion | Less than 100g CO2 eg/kWh | Less than 100g CO2 eg/kWh | Above 50 MW eligible | | | |

### Solar power generation

On-shore solar power generation is eligible in all frameworks. The EU taxonomy uses its standard threshold of 100 gr CO2e per kWh for electricity generation. According to the CBI taxonomy criterion, an on-shore solar power generation activity is eligible if no more than 15% of power generation in the facility comes from non-renewable sources. There are no specific thresholds in the other frameworks as reviewed.

**Table 4.3. Solar power criteria across jurisdictions**

| Solar or shore Photovoltaic and C SP* | CBI Taxonomy | EU Taxonomy | China Definitions | Japan Definitions | France Definitions | Netherlands Definitions |
|---|---|---|---|---|---|---|
| Included (yes/no) | Yes | Yes | Yes | Yes | Yes | yes |
| Criterion | Less than 15% of electricity generated from non RE* sources | Less than 100g CO2 eg/kWh declining to net-zero in 2050 | | CBI | CBI | |

### Wind power generation

On-shore wind power generation is eligible in all frameworks. The EU taxonomy uses its standard threshold of 100 gr CO2e per kWh for electricity generation, while CBI allows the activity if no more than 15% of power generation in the facility comes from non-renewable sources. There are no specific thresholds in the other frameworks as reviewed.

**Table 4.4. Wind power criteria across jurisdictions**

| On shore Wind | CBI Taxonomy | EU Taxonomy | China Definitions | Japan Definitions | France Definitions | Netherlands Definitions |
|---|---|---|---|---|---|---|
| Included (yes/no) | Yes | Yes | Yes | Yes | Yes | yes |
| Criterion | Less than 15% of electricity generated from non RE* sources | Less than 100g CO2 eg/kWh declining to net-zero in 2050 | | CBI | CBI | |

### Green building construction

Green building construction is eligible in all frameworks, but criteria vary. In the European Union, the Nearly Zero Energy Buildings Directive (NZEB) sets the standards from 2020 onwards. Both the CBI and the EU Taxonomy restrict eligibility to a version of best-in class: top 15% of performers in the local market in terms of emissions footprint (CBI), or buildings with primary energy demand 20% lower than NZEB (EU Taxonomy). In Japan, to be certified, green buildings must meet national level standards such as LEED and CASBEE. In China, there are standards for construction of green buildings at local level (province or city).

Table 4.5. Green building construction criteria across jurisdictions

| Green buildings constructions | CBI Taxonomy | EU Taxonomy | China Definitions | Japan Definitions | France Definitions | Netherlands Definitions |
|---|---|---|---|---|---|---|
| Included (yes/no) | Yes | Yes | Yes | Yes | Yes | yes |
| Criterion | Emissions footprint in top 15% of the local market | Primary energy demand in kWh/m2/year at least 20% lower than NZEB* | Regional/City level standards | National standards eg LEEDS* and CASBEE* | CBI | NZEB* for new build after 2020 |

*Green building renovation*

Green building renovation is eligible in all frameworks, but criteria vary. In the European Union, the Energy Performance Buildings Directive (EPBD) revised in 2018 is the reference standard. CBI allows the choice of a standard of relative performance (the top 15% best performers in the local market, based on emissions footprint), or absolute performance (the retrofit results in a "substantial reduction" in emissions). Similarly, the EU Taxonomy provides a choice: renovations either can bring buildings in line with EPBD requirements, or must achieve a reduction of at least 30% in primary energy demand. In Japan, national level standards such as LEEDs and CASBEE are used, and there are standards set at the level of regional or city authorities in China.

Table 4.6. Green building renovation criteria across jurisdictions

| Green buildings renovation | CBI Taxonomy | EU Taxonomy | China Definitions | Japan Definitions | France Definitions | Netherlands Definitions |
|---|---|---|---|---|---|---|
| Included (yes/no) | Yes | Yes | Yes | Yes | Yes | yes |
| Criterion | Emissions footprint in top 15% of the local market or substantial reduction in gr Co2/m2 due to retrofit | Primary energy demand consistent with EPBD* for major renovation, or 30% reduction in Primary energy demand for relative improvement | Regional/City level standards | National standards eg LEEDS* and CASBEE* | CBI | EPBD* |

## 4.3. Differences

Three sectors -- non-renewable power generation, transport and manufacturing -- are covered in certain definitions but not in others. In the case of non-renewable power generation, there are varying approaches with respect to inclusion or exclusion of nuclear power, of gas fired power, and of supercritical coal fired power. For transport, some frameworks include aviation and shipping and others do not. For manufacturing, some frameworks include the transition of hard-to-abate sectors such as cement or steel manufacturing, while others do not. Those differences are mapped in more detail below.

### 4.3.1. Non-renewable power generation

The jurisdictions in scope vary significantly with respect to inclusion of non-renewable power generation, i.e. nuclear and fossil fuel based power generation. China appears to be the most inclusive. With respect to nuclear energy, the 2019 Guiding Catalogue for the Green Industry issued by the NDRC[2] mentions the manufacture of nuclear power facilities as eligible under "clean energy Industry"[3]. Nuclear power generation is also eligible under the CBI taxonomy. Its status under the EU Taxonomy is subject to further study by the TEG or the Platform that the EC will set up as an advisory body on the Taxonomy Regulation and its implementation after the TEG dissolves in September 2020. In particular, further study will determine whether nuclear waste generation and treatment is compatible with the Do No Significant Harm requirement[4]. The French GreenFin Label excludes nuclear power generation and the nuclear value chain. There is no mention of nuclear power generation in the Japanese and Dutch definitions[5].

With respect to gas, the Chinese NDRC green industry catalogue of 2019 includes "manufacture of unconventional gas exploration facilities" under "clean energy". Furthermore, construction and operation of natural gas transmission, storage and load regulation facilities is included under "efficient operation of the energy system". Gas fired power generation is not eligible under the CBI taxonomy framework. In the EU Taxonomy, gas fired power generation is eligible only if it meets the 100g CO2 e /kWh threshold in the EU Taxonomy. There is no gas eligibility in the other frameworks.

Regarding coal, the Chinese NDRC green industry catalogue mentions clean production and utilization of coal (under "clean and efficient utilization of traditional energy") and upgrade and operation of coal-fired power generation units for flexible load regulation (under "efficient operation of the energy system"). No further specification of the technology is available at this stage. China is the only jurisdiction in scope where coal fired power is present in sustainable finance definitions.

The rationale for including ultra-supercritical coal in the NDRC green industry catalogue may have been its expected effectiveness in reducing particle air pollution for instance in places like Beijing. In May 2020 the press (Financial Times, 2020[2]) reported that a new green industry catalogue was published for consultation by the PBOC. This catalogue is available only in Chinese at the time of writing and was not consulted directly. The industry reports that the new version of the catalogue excludes coal and the production or utilization of natural gas. The catalogue was jointly issued by the PBOC, the securities regulator and the NDRC. It was announced that all financial sector regulators will be using the new catalogue.

Table 4.7. Non-renewable power generation inclusions across jurisdictions

| Non renewable power generation Included (yes/no) | CBI Taxonomy | EU Taxonomy | China Definitions | Japan Definitions | France Definitions | Netherlands Definitions |
|---|---|---|---|---|---|---|
| Nuclear | Yes | No | Yes | No | No | No |
| Gas | No | Yes With emissions threshold | Yes | No | No | No |
| "Clean coal" | No | No | Yes | No | No | No |

### 4.3.2. Transport

All frameworks in scope specify that private and public passenger transport and rail freight are eligible activities. All frameworks cover waterborne transport, but in the case of the EU taxonomy, only inland water transport, not international shipping, is covered. Aviation for its part is covered only in the CBI and Japanese frameworks.

EU taxonomy criteria are generally more stringent than CBI criteria for private and public passenger or road or rail freight transport. CBI automatically accepts electric and hydrogen vehicles, including trains. For freight rail, CBI requires that no more than 50% of transported freight should be fossil. For vehicles, the EU taxonomy uses a zero tailpipe emissions criterion, with a phase-in; a maximum of 50 g CO2 e per passenger- km is admitted until 2025. The same criterion applies to passenger rail. For freight rail, the criterion is 50% lower than average reference CO2 emissions of heavy duty vehicles (HDVs) as defined for the Heavy Duty CO2 Regulation. Rail that is dedicated to the transport of fossil fuels is excluded.

Regarding cargo or passenger vessels, the CBI criterion for inclusion is "the use of low GHG fuel delivering substantial reduction in emissions per passenger or tonne per kilometre". The EU Taxonomy criterion (which applies only to inland water transport) is more stringent, with a direct emissions requirement below 95g CO2 e per passenger-km for passenger waterborne transport. For freight (i.e. cargo) vessels, only zero-direct-emissions vessels are eligible, or those with direct CO2e emissions per tonne kilometre 50% lower than the average reference value defined for HDVs (Heavy Duty CO2 Regulation). Freight vessels used for fossil fuel transportation are excluded.

Regarding aviation, CBI's criterion is the use of a low GHG emitting fuel, delivering substantial emissions reductions. The EU has not yet developed criteria for aviation. In Japan and France, sustainable finance definitions for aviation make reference to the CBI taxonomy.

Table 4.8. Transport inclusions across jurisdictions

| Transport Included (yes/no) | CBI Taxonomy | EU Taxonomy | China Definitions | Japan Definitions | France Definitions | Netherlands Definitions |
|---|---|---|---|---|---|---|
| Private passenger | Yes | Yes | Yes | Yes | Yes | Yes |
| Public passenger | Yes | Yes | Yes | Yes | Yes | Yes |
| Freight rail | Yes | Yes | Yes | Yes | Yes | Yes |
| Aviation | Yes | No | No | Yes | Yes | No |
| Waterborne | Yes | Inland only | Yes | Yes | Yes | Yes |

### 4.3.3. Manufacturing

The EU Taxonomy recognizes that some hard-to-abate industrial activities are necessary to supply the building of a low-carbon economy that will be compliant with the EU net-zero objective in 2050. Such activities are included as "transition activities" in the EU Taxonomy.

The EU's reference point for manufacturing sector criteria has been the EU-Emissions Trading Scheme (ETS) benchmarks. For plants producing only cement clinker, as of February 2020, the EU-ETS benchmark value for cement clinker manufacturing is 0.766 tCO2e/t of clinker. Under the Taxonomy, plants emitting below this threshold are eligible. For plants producing clinker and cement, the specific emissions associated with the clinker and cement production processes must be lower than 0.498 of tCO2e/t cement or alternative binder.

Manufacture of primary aluminium is eligible if Criterion 1 is met in combination with either Criterion 2 or 3 below.

- Criterion 1: Direct emissions for primary aluminium production is at or below the value of the related EU-ETS benchmark. As of February 2020, the EU-ETS benchmark value for aluminium manufacturing is 1.514 $tCO_2e/t$.
- Criterion 2: Electricity consumption for electrolysis is at or below 15.29 MWh/t (European average emission factor according to International Aluminium Institute, 2017, to be updated annually) (International Aluminium Institute, 2017[3])
- Criterion 3: Average carbon intensity of the electricity that is used for primary aluminium production (electrolysis) is at or below 100 g $CO_2e/kWh$.

Manufacturing of iron and steel is eligible if the GHG emissions associated with the production processes are lower than the values of the related EU-ETS benchmarks. As of February 2020, the EU-ETS benchmarks values for iron and steel manufacturing are, for hot metal, 1.328 $tCO_2e/t$ product, and for sintered ore, 0.171 $tCO_2e/t$ product.

For hydrogen, the criteria are threefold:

- Direct $CO_2$ emissions from manufacturing of hydrogen is at or below 5.8 $tCO_2e/t$ Hydrogen, in alignment with energy thresholds in the EU taxonomy.
- Electricity use for hydrogen produced by electrolysis is at or lower than 58 MWh/t Hydrogen.
- Average carbon intensity of the electricity produced and used for hydrogen manufacturing is at or below 100 g $CO_2e/kWh$.

Only the EU Taxonomy has criteria in the manufacturing sector:

### Table 4.9. Inclusion of the manufacturing sector across taxonomies

| Manufacturing Included (yes/no) | CBI Taxonomy | EU Taxonomy | China Definitions | Japan Definitions | France Definitions | Netherlands Definitions |
|---|---|---|---|---|---|---|
| **Cement** | No | Yes | No | No | No | No |
| **Aluminium** | No | Yes | No | No | No | No |
| **Iron and Steel** | No | Yes | No | No | No | No |
| **Hydrogen** | No | No | No | No | No | No |

## 4.4. Gaps: sectors not covered in any of the definitions in scope

Some sectors of the economy are not covered by any of the sustainable finance definitions and taxonomies examined. Many of the frameworks are still relatively new and under development. For instance, both the EU and China have indicated their intention to update and possibly expand their respective frameworks to include new sectors in the coming months or years. It also is worth noting that these frameworks were developed before the occurrence of the Covid-19 pandemic and the resulting economic shock. New policy emergencies may arise in the future that could spur opportunities and actions to design principles and metrics for the inclusion of new sectors in sustainable finance taxonomies.

A case in point is aviation. Before the Covid-19 crisis, the EU had signalled its intention to consider eligibility criteria for the aviation sector in the Taxonomy in the coming years. Now, the aviation sector is a candidate for rescue finance packages in many jurisdictions, as governments attempt to address the economic impact of the lockdown. Important investments are needed to ensure an economic recovery, including by the private sector. The selection of criteria for the aviation sector in the Taxonomy could provide a basis for specifying setting sustainability-linked conditions for rescue financing for the aviation sector.

In the same vein, it is worth noting that the health sector is absent from all the frameworks covered by the present report. The pandemic situation may lead to additional investment in the health sector. In that context, the EU may wish to establish sustainability criteria for such investments.

The present economic context illustrates the fact that the emerging field of sustainable finance definitions is still a work in process, and needs to be adaptable as investment needs shift with economic and policy emergencies. At the same time, the overarching goal of putting economies on sustainable pathways cannot be lost from sight, given the degree of urgency of environmental issues.

In this respect, it is worth noting that none of the frameworks specifically covers so-called brown activities. As noted in the second part of this report, first chapter, paragraph 189, the EC signalled its intention to develop a brown taxonomy in the coming years. None of the frameworks specifically considers a "transition" taxonomy, although the EU Taxonomy includes enabling activities and activities in the process of becoming green (as described in Chapter 7 of this report). At the same time, a number of financial institutions have issued so-called "transition bonds" as an instrument to finance the decarbonisation of high emitting companies. The International Capital Markets Association (ICMA), which shepherded the development of the Green Bond Principles, has established a Working Group on Climate Transition Finance, which may be expected to develop principles or guidelines for transition bonds. In light of these developments, "brown" and "transition" definitions relevant to sustainable finance could increasingly become part of the collective policy toolbox in the future.

## 4.5. Conclusions of the comparison

Keeping in mind the essential differences outlined in section 4.1, the sustainable finance taxonomies and definitions in scope are largely similar for renewable energy and green buildings. In those sectors, international investors can find a common language in existing legal definitions across jurisdictions. By contrast, in non-renewable power generation and transport, international investors will find that sectoral coverage is similar across jurisdictions but criteria for inclusion differ. The EU taxonomy is unique in its inclusion of some hard-to-abate manufacturing sectors such as cement, steel, aluminium and hydrogen, all in relation to the EU ETS mechanism for identifying the best environmental performers. Other frameworks do not include such sectors.

Finally, some sectors are not covered in any of the frameworks under consideration, such as health or aviation. Following the economic consequences of the Covid-19 lockdown, and massive additional investment in those two sectors, among others, it may be worth considering criteria under which investment in these sectors could be defined as environmentally sustainable.

## References

European Commission (2020), *https://ec.europa.eu/growth/sectors/raw-materials/industries/forest-based/sustainable-forest-management_en*. [1]

Financial Times (2020), *https://www.ft.com/content/253f969c-37e0-42cd-9cdf-e06a5262fffe*. [2]

International Aluminium Institute (2017), *http://www.world-aluminium.org/statistics/primary-aluminium-smelting-power-consumption/#data*. [3]

## Notes

[1] Such as Forest Stewardship Council (FSC) or Programme for the Endorsement of Forest Certification (PEFC).

[2] Based on an unofficial translation into English kindly provided by CBI. Also, refer to chapter "Sustainable finance definitions and taxonomies in China".

[3] Section 3.1.5 of the catalogue.

[4] See chapter 7 EU sustainable finance taxonomy.

[5] It was therefore considered that nuclear is excluded from these definitions.

# 5 Preliminary reflections on policy considerations relevant to sustainable finance definitions and taxonomies

This chapter proposes initial policy considerations relevant to the design of sustainable finance taxonomies by policy makers. For instance, taxonomies can deal with economic activities, or with financial products. They can cover a variety of environmental objectives. They can target different "shades of green", ranging from activities that are already aligned with environmental objectives, to transition activities, even to "dirty" activities at the opposite end of the spectrum. The stringency of criteria, geographical scope, and adaptability to innovation are additional examples of design considerations.

This chapter proposes elements for policy makers to consider in relation to the design and implementation of sustainable finance taxonomies and definitions. In the rest of this section, references to "taxonomies" should be understood as referring to both taxonomies and definitions – i.e. policies, regulations or official guidance defining sustainable finance activities or products comprehensively in a given jurisdiction[1]. Gathering and expanding ideas from previous sections, this section puts forward a preliminary set of issues for examination in future research. This future work will aim to provide evidence-based research to support policy makers' efforts to design and implement sustainable finance taxonomies. In the meantime, this section can serve as an initial checklist of issues and options for policy makers to consider.

## 5.1. Taxonomy design issues: role of taxonomies in the achievement of environmental policy objectives

### *5.1.1. Overarching objectives of a sustainable finance taxonomy*

The design of a taxonomy will depend on its objectives. One objective may be to help the flow of investment capital to a sustainable economy, with the definition of "sustainable economy" influencing the taxonomy design (see discussion below on "environmental objectives"). An additional objective may be to increase market confidence by avoiding green washing. A third objective may be to measure the stocks or flow of sustainable investments in the economy to assess them against specific objectives (e.g. "two-degree alignment"). Taxonomies can also be used as a basis to develop a system of incentives for sustainable finance. Such incentives can be designed in monetary policy (such as lower refinancing rates for banks on green lending, a policy implemented in China). They can be designed in fiscal policy (such as reduced tax rates on green loans, a policy in the Netherlands), or in financial policy (such as interest rate reduction for green loans, also in place in the Netherlands).

### *5.1.2. Sustainable finance economic activities versus sustainable financial products*

The EU has chosen to establish a taxonomy for economic activities based on NACE codes. By contrast, some other jurisdictions such as China and the Netherlands have established taxonomies based on sustainable finance products (such as green loans or green investment funds). In the EU, future legislation will be developed to reference the EU Taxonomy in sustainable finance products definitions such as green investment funds (EU Ecolabel for retail funds and EU Green Bond Standard). Not all issuers or investors in the EU have been using the NACE code framework, so the use of this framework will require some adaptation by the market that will be key to the fast and successful implementation of the EU taxonomy.

### *5.1.3. Environmental and other objectives*

A taxonomy can cover many objectives. They range from climate mitigation to other environmental objectives -- such as climate adaptation, circular economy, sustainable use and protection of water and marine resources, waste prevention and recycling, pollution prevention control and protection of healthy ecosystems -- to social and governance objectives, as in the EU taxonomy. Such objectives can be considered as independent (such as in China), or can be interlinked, as in the EU, based on the concepts of substantial contribution and do no significant harm.

The scope and level of ambition of the taxonomy will influence its complexity, the costs of implementation and supervision and the ease and pace of uptake by the market. In these respects, the beginning of market implementation of the EU taxonomy in the coming months will provide opportunity for market feedback. The EU taxonomy will be referenced in several forthcoming regulations or directives at EU level, including the EU Green Bond Standard, the EU Ecolabel, the revised Non Financial Reporting Directive and others. The introduction of the taxonomy in these frameworks will influence the way issuers and investors report on environmental sustainability and will enable to assess the effective complexity, costs and opportunities of providing taxonomy alignment related data.

Further issues for consideration include ways to design a "social" taxonomy, or to design social dimensions to a taxonomy also covering environmental issues. The EU is the only jurisdiction in the scope of this report that has attempted to incorporate social issues using a "minimum safeguards" approach based on existing international frameworks such as the OECD MNE guidelines, ILO and UN conventions. Other approaches could be envisaged bringing focus on specific social goals such as gender equality or others.

### 5.1.4. "Binary taxonomy", "transition" and "brown taxonomies"

Taxonomies in scope of this report attempt to identify what is sustainable or green. By doing so, they serve as an instrument for identifying investment opportunities. Beyond opportunities, issuers and investors also are increasingly focused on the risks posed to their activities and performance by climate change and other sustainability issues such as biodiversity loss. Therefore, a "brown taxonomy" identifying which activities are detrimental to sustainability objectives, could be useful from a risk perspective. It also would be useful to investors seeking to shift their investments away from activities that are less environmentally sustainable. The EU has indicated that it would consider developing a brown taxonomy and provide a first report on a taxonomy for environmentally harmful activities by the end of 2021.

Another way to design a taxonomy could be to provide a comprehensive, "multi-colour" screening system that would enable the ranking of a whole portfolio from "pure green" to "dark brown", and any activities that might be characterised by other colours (e.g. those with ambiguous or no climate implications, such as the health or media sectors). The EU approach remains a binary approach (economic activities are either compliant with the sustainability standard or they are not). However, "transition" and "enabling" activities have been included in the framework. The EU taxonomy therefore aims to include not only activities that are already "green", but also activities which are on a transition pathway, and activities enabling others to exist such as essential parts of their supply chain. . The link of taxonomies to transitions also needs to be framed within a systems approach that allows for multiple pathways.

### 5.1.5. Systems approach

Based on the OECD contribution to the TEG, the EU taxonomy incorporates the notion of a systems approach to economic activities. This approach recognizes that an economic activity cannot be considered truly sustainable independent of the wider system in which it operates. For instance, the contribution of electric vehicles to environmental sustainability should be assessed not only against their own emissions characteristics, but also against the wider benefits that they may or may not provide in terms of traffic congestion, within a transport system that takes into consideration land use and alternative mobility options. Consistent with this notion, the taxonomy identifies activities that make a substantial contribution on their own but also enable the overall transition of critical systems such as the energy, transport, urban, water and food systems. A taxonomy-eligible activity may only contribute to an individual country or region's transition pathway when it is also coherent with the transition of the overall system of which the activity is a part. Awareness of systems issues on the part of market actors and policymakers can and should lead to innovation, new thinking on eligibility criteria for certain activities, and updated criteria .

### 5.1.6. Integrating pathways in the design of taxonomies

The EU taxonomy screens a number of activities based not only on a threshold to meet today, but also on a future trajectory that the activity must follow in order to reach the sectoral, climate and environmental objectives agreed at EU level. The policy objective referenced most often in the current version of the EU taxonomy is reaching carbon neutrality by 2050. Other jurisdictions have different long-term climate policy objectives and will follow different pathways, which could be reflected in their sustainable finance definitions and taxonomies. Integrating pathways into definitions and taxonomies can help avoid lock-in of emitting activities and assets, and help ensure that eligible investments will be compatible with long-term policy objectives. However, pathways have a number of complexities and raise several issues. One is that there are many potential (global) emissions pathways to a given goal. Choosing one of them for the taxonomy requires careful consideration of implications. A second issue worth considering here is that different countries will opt for different transition pathways. A third issue is that if a pathway can be identified for a given economic activity, an approach is still needed to translate the pathway or pathways to the level of a corporate.

### *5.1.7. Stringency of criteria*

The choice of stringency in thresholds is a key element in the design of a sustainable finance taxonomy. Less stringent thresholds favour the uptake of a taxonomy by issuers of green financial products, for whom it will be easier to find taxonomy-compliant projects. Thresholds that are more stringent may give more confidence to investors in asserting the environmental benefits of their investments. They also may channel capital faster to ambitious green activities (but perhaps less capital overall than would be channelled by less stringent thresholds).

### *5.1.8. Adapting to innovation and technology developments*

A taxonomy should be able to adapt to the emergence of new technologies. Consequently, a challenge of designing a taxonomy is the need to ensure sufficiently frequent updates to minimise any lag behind market innovation. Setting ambitious thresholds in a taxonomy framework can itself spur innovation, by inciting corporates to better their environmental performance to match the threshold.

## 5.2. Role of taxonomies for issuers and investors: Taxonomy usability and implementation issues

### *5.2.1. Geographical scope*

In today's globalised economy, underpinned by global financial systems, many issuers and investors will have activities and investments across several jurisdictions. A taxonomy reflecting only a single jurisdiction and its associated activities will not be sufficient to enable issues and investors to cover all of their international activities or investments. In order to resolve this issue, the TEG has identified certain criteria in the EU taxonomy as being of "international relevance", meaning that users of the taxonomy could use them for economic activities located outside the EU. Criteria for sustainable forest management, for example, are designated as being of international relevance[2].

For some sectors, there is no consistency between various taxonomies, as the mapping in section 4 suggests. For instance, the manufacturing of cement and steel would be eligible under certain conditions in the EU Taxonomy, and not in other taxonomies considered in this report. There are differences between taxonomies on environmental objectives and the link between them, sectoral coverage, thresholds and exclusions. The EU has sought to address this in part by having some criteria of international relevance. It has also set up the International Platform on Sustainable Finance (IPSF) as a platform to exchange and disseminate best practices in environmentally sustainable finance, to compare different initiatives and identify barriers and opportunities to help scale up environmentally sustainable finance internationally. The Platform also aims at enhancing international cooperation where appropriate, while respecting national and international contexts. Cooperation creates the potential for reducing differences.

### 5.2.2. Data availability

The introduction of government-sponsored sustainable finance taxonomies may significantly increase demand for data from issuers and investors in order to check eligibility of activities and/or investments. The issue of data availability is central to the uptake of taxonomies. Just as there are many different definitions of green finance, there is also a variety of methodologies for reporting certain metrics, such as carbon emissions. According to how taxonomies and other sustainable finance regulations, such as disclosure requirements, are designed, data may need to be provided by issuers (including corporates), by investors, or by both. Data may be provided by issuers' and investors' in-house resources, or by third-party specialized data provision firms, to which issuers and investors outsource data production.

The implementation of taxonomies requires a degree of standardisation of the data provided, to allow for aggregation and assessment of compliance in a way that is consistent and comparable. The extent of this need for data, and possible gaps compared to presently available data, depends on the design of the taxonomy. While the production of data will absorb financial and labour resources, it is necessary to enable the assessment of investors or issuers against sustainability objectives. There could be important trade-offs in terms of uptake of taxonomies if taxonomy design leads to persistent data needs and gaps. Active and ongoing efforts by various initiatives (e.g. by the Principles for Responsible Investment, PRI, or the United Nations Environmental Programme Finance Initiative, UNEP FI) to test how the EU taxonomy will be implemented by users, will help to identify challenges with respect to data availability.

### 5.2.3. Data verification

Compliance with sustainable finance taxonomies may need to be verified by third parties. Such third parties may be accredited professional verifiers, such as is envisaged for the EU Green Bond Standard. Market supervisors and regulatory authorities may also play a role in the supervision of implementation of taxonomy frameworks. The existence of taxonomies in itself is no guarantee that greenwashing will not take place, because financial market participants or corporates could report compliance inaccurately. Therefore, the quality of the verification process of a taxonomy will be particularly important to reduce the risk of green- and impact-washing, and thereby to provide confidence that will enable market growth. The nature of data certification and verification is also a determinant of the liability risks associated with inaccurate data provision, and potentially with investments made on the basis of sustainable finance credentials. Data verification is therefore an important part of the architecture and implementation of taxonomies.

### 5.2.4. Usability

The likely "ease of use" of a taxonomy for its intended users is an important consideration when designing a taxonomy. This is particularly true at present, when economies worldwide are coping with economic and financial impacts and pressures created by COVID-19 response measures, and financial and human resources may be constrained to incorporate new frameworks. In the case of the EU taxonomy, a degree of complexity results from the use of economic activities and NACE codes as the core structure of the taxonomy, because NACE codes are not always consistent with accounting frameworks used by corporates. Another degree of complexity derives from the EU's ambition to interlink six environmental objectives together through the "do no significant harm" approach, thereby requiring six types of assessment for every single economic activity. The EU taxonomy has not yet been implemented in practice, and important considerations in terms of usability will come out of its effective implementation. A related consideration for taxonomy design is to involve final users at an early stage in the legislative process. Several consultations are now on going at EC level to that effect regarding the EU taxonomy.

### *5.2.5. Proportionality*

Sustainability objectives need to be embedded across the global economy, not only for large issuers and investors but also for smaller operators. An important usability consideration is to make taxonomy compliance achievable for smaller corporates and financial market participants. This may involve using a proportionality approach when designing compliance and verification criteria. The Netherlands for instance has developed successfully green loans and funds schemes tailored to retail markets and small businesses, including not only specific incentives for small-sized operation but also a distribution system involving retail banking networks.

## Notes

[1] This excludes definitions that do not apply beyond a single instrument such as a green bond or a green investment fund.

[2] Please refer to paragraph 289 in the Annex regarding EU taxonomy forestry criteria.

# 6 Conclusion

If appropriately designed, taxonomies can play a useful role in the architecture of countries financial systems, in order to channel and accelerate sustainable investment flows. In terms of common principles and metrics, keeping in mind the specific features of the EU taxonomy, similarities exist between the official definitions of sustainable finance scoped in this report.

In the five jurisdictions examined in this report -- China, the EU, Japan, France and the Netherlands -- the level of development of sustainable finance taxonomies and definitions established under law varies. Some jurisdictions have a precise nomenclature of legally defined sustainable finance products, in some cases with incentives. In other jurisdictions, like in the EU, this may be part of future developments.

The EU taxonomy, which is still under development, is unique in at least three ways. First, it interlinks six environmental objectives based on the "Do No Significant Harm" principle. Second, it makes room for transition and enabling activities, with thresholds declining over time. Third, it includes some hard-to-abate manufacturing sectors such as cement, steel, aluminium and hydrogen, all in relation to the EU ETS mechanism for identifying the best environmental performers.

Keeping in mind the unique aspects of the EU Taxonomy, the sustainable finance taxonomies and definitions in scope are largely similar for renewable power generation and green buildings. In those sectors, international investors can find a common language in existing legal definitions across jurisdictions. In non-renewable power generation and transport, international investors will find that sectoral coverage is similar across jurisdictions, but criteria for inclusion differ. None of the considered frameworks proposes an exhaustive sectoral framework: several important sectors of the economy are missing, such as aviation, maritime transport, health or the agro-food business. Sustainable finance taxonomies serve, in part, to signal where investment is needed to achieve the goals of the Paris Agreement and the SDGs. Accordingly, taxonomies may expand to cover currently missing sectors, as they will require investment in coming years to reach sustainability objectives.

The EU Taxonomy has triggered interest in various jurisdictions to consider developing sustainable finance taxonomies, which can play a useful role in the architecture of a sustainable finance system. In particular, taxonomies can help avoid green washing, reduce market fragmentation, and accelerate the flow of investment to sustainable economic activities. Taxonomies can serve as a basis to develop incentives for channelling investments to desired objectives. They can also facilitate the monitoring of such flows.

In order to serve their purpose effectively, taxonomies need to be properly designed. Based on the examination of the five taxonomies in this report, key aspects have been identified for consideration by policy makers. A first set of considerations relates to the environmental and other objectives linked to taxonomies. Such objectives can range from climate to environmental, social and governance objectives. A taxonomy identifies activities that are already "green", but can also identify activities in transition and even "brown" activities. It should use a system approach as a basis to inform the identification of eligible economic activities, and to take into account the different pathways that can lead to the desired longer-term environmental goal. It also should be able to adapt to innovation and technological development. A second set of considerations pertains to the usability of a taxonomy for its end users, issuers and investors. Ease of use is an important consideration for quick and efficient market uptake. Data availability and verification are key aspects, as well as proportionality.

While taxonomies may be designed initially to serve domestic or regional environmental objectives, they will be used by global corporate and financial actors, with activities and investment across various jurisdictions. To enhance international dialogue and cooperation on taxonomies, the EU has initiated a Platform, to which the OECD is an observer. Going forward, disseminating knowledge and guidance for best practice in taxonomy design can support countries in developing such taxonomies. It also can facilitate international cooperation by harmonising principles and approaches where feasible and desirable, while taking into account the specific contexts and transition trajectories as needed. These areas are proposed as a direction for future research.

# Part II Developing sustainable finance definitions and taxonomies

# 7 The European Union sustainable finance taxonomy

The EU taxonomy regulation was published in June 2020. It defines sustainable economic activities as those providing a substantial contribution to one of six environmental objectives: climate change mitigation, adaptation, protection of water, ecosystems, circular economy and tackling pollution. At the same time, such substantial contribution on one objective must go with not significantly harming any other objective. The EU taxonomy regulation will be an essential reference in a number of other forthcoming sustainable finance regulations in the EU, such as those addressing disclosures or the EU green bond standard. The EU Technical Expert Group has proposed Technical Screening Criteria to the Commission; those will be considered for inclusion in a forthcoming legislation by the end of 2020.

## 7.1. History and present status of EU taxonomy

### *7.1.1. Introduction*

In March 2018, the European Commission (EC) put forward a draft "Regulation on the establishment of a framework to facilitate sustainable investment" (EuropeanCommission, 2018[1]). This regulation set out a framework for designing a taxonomy of environmentally sustainable economic activities. In doing so, the EC followed the recommendation of the High Level Expert Group on Sustainable Finance (HLEG), an expert group established by the EC in December 2016. The HLEG had a mandate to develop a comprehensive European strategy on green finance . In June 2018, the EC appointed a Technical Expert Group (the TEG) to, among other things, help it design the technical screening criteria for the taxonomy. The OECD was an observer to the TEG. In parallel, a Member States Expert Group was also established. These groups initiated discussions, both at state level and in financial markets, on whether it was appropriate to legislate on a taxonomy, and if so how [the taxonomy should be designed. The outcome of these discussions was the adoption of the taxonomy regulation by EU co-legislators (European Commission, European Parliament and Council of Europe) in December 2019. The EC also launched an International Platform on Sustainable Finance (IPSF) in September 2019 as a way to facilitate the exchange of views on best practices, promote international cooperation and, when appropriate, coordination in the area of environmentally sustainable finance.

### *7.1.2. The High Level Expert Group on Sustainable Finance*

As part of its effort to tackle the climate challenge, the European Commission signalled its intention to spur the development of sustainable finance, as part of the completion of the Capital Markets Union led by DG FISMA. Appointed in 2016, the EU High Level Expert Group (HLEG) on Sustainable Finance recommended ten priority actions to the Commission. The first point was to develop "a common sustainable finance taxonomy to ensure market consistency and clarity, starting with climate change." The final report of the HLEG report stated that "if Europe is to mobilise capital at scale for sustainable development, it needs a technically robust classification system to establish market clarity on what is 'green' or 'sustainable'. Introducing a sustainability taxonomy will enhance market efficiency and help to channel capital flows towards assets that contribute to sustainable development" (HLEG, 2018[1]). In March 2018, against the backdrop of the HLEG's recommendations, the EC published its Action Plan on Financing Sustainable Growth. In May, a legislative proposal on the establishment of a taxonomy for environmentally sustainable economic activities ensued. The EC nominated a Technical Expert Group (TEG) to assist in the development of that legislative proposal, with the OECD as an observer.

### *7.1.3. Role of the TEG*

The TEG is a group of 35 members mostly from the financial industry, asset management firms, development banks, trade associations and NGOs. The European Bank for Reconstruction and Development (EBRD), the Central Bank Network for Greening the Financial System (NGFS), the United Nations Environment Programme Finance Initiative (UNEP FI) and OECD are observers. The group's initial term was one year and was subsequently extended to September 2020. The group met physically in Brussels for an average of two days per month. The TEG was divided into four sub-groups, with three corresponding to each of three regulations (taxonomy, benchmarks for the asset management industry, climate related disclosures), and a fourth tasked with making recommendations on a possible future standard for EU-labelled Green Bonds. Regarding the Taxonomy Regulation, the TEG's role has been to assist the Commission in preparing the Delegated Acts for the draft regulation issued by the Commission in March 2018. The Delegated Acts will contain the details for implementing the regulation, called Technical Screening Criteria. The regulation will enter into force as the Delegated Acts and associated Technical Screening Criteria are issued in stages between 2022 and 2023. The TEG consulted extensively with the public and a wide range of experts during its mandate. In March 2020, the TEG issued its final summary report on the Taxonomy Regulation, a technical annex and an excel tool.

### *7.1.4. Next legislative steps*

European co-legislators adopted the Taxonomy Regulation (henceforth "the Regulation") on December 18, 2019. The Regulation was published at the Official Journal of the European Union on June 20, 2020 (EUOFFICIALJOURNAL, 2020[2]). The Regulation establishes a step-by step process, where Technical Screening Criteria are adopted in two batches of Delegated Acts. The first batch concerns climate change adaptation and mitigation (see below for a description of environmental objectives in the Regulation). They must be adopted by 31 December 2020, for entry into application on 31 December 2021. The second batch concerns the four other environmental objectives established in the Regulation (water, waste, pollution and ecosystems). They must be adopted one year later, i.e. by 31 December 2021 for entry into application on 31 December 2022.

The May 2018 legislative proposal "establishes the criteria for determining whether an economic activity is environmentally sustainable"[1]. Therefore, the Regulation does not deal with financial products. The EC is currently working on a legislative proposal for an EU Ecolabel for retail financial products. The EU Ecolabel is expected to make reference to the Taxonomy. The TEG also issued a Usability Guide for the EU Green Bond Standard at the same time as the final Taxonomy report. The EU Green Bond Standard (EU GBS) is a TEG recommendation to the EC for an EU label for Green Bonds. The draft model of the EU GBS in the TEG's final report would link use-of-proceeds of EU Green Bonds to the EU Taxonomy Regulation. It also calls for mandatory verification by accredited verifiers.

To sum up, the EU taxonomy as available now is an existing regulation, but is not yet implemented nor fully developed. Besides, it sets a framework to define environmentally sustainable economic activities, but does not apply directly to financial products.

## 7.2. Objectives and scope of the EU Taxonomy

### *7.2.1. Objectives*

The EU Taxonomy's objectives are linked to those of the EC Action Plan on Financing Sustainable Growth, published in March 2018:

- Reorient capital flows towards sustainable investment, in order to achieve sustainable and inclusive growth,
- Manage financial risks stemming from climate change, environmental degradation and social issues,
- Foster transparency and long-termism in financial and economic activity.

The EU Taxonomy aims at being a classification system that provides a common language on what constitutes a sustainable activity, i.e. the criteria an economic activity must meet to qualify as contributing to EU sustainability objectives. Establishing the classification system can help achieve goals such as fostering transparency and reorienting cash flows toward sustainable investment. At the time, , there was no such classification system at EU level (there is one now), and existing market-based practices are not necessarily aligned with EU environmental and sustainability policy objectives. Furthermore, national standards and financial product labels within the EU differ, which might be warranted on some grounds, but also might in some cases confuse investors, including retail investors. Differences between national standards and labels in some cases also could hamper cross-border sustainable investments. Incoherence between classification systems or the absence of classification system in some jurisdictions might also create the risk of greenwashing, which could undermine investors' confidence.

### 7.2.2. Scope/ Activities

The EU legislators aimed at a definition of sustainability that goes beyond climate objectives, and encompasses social and governance aspects. The six environmental objectives identified for the EU Taxonomy are:

1. Climate change mitigation
2. Climate change adaptation
3. Sustainable use and protection of water and marine resources
4. Transition to a circular economy
5. Pollution prevention and control
6. Protection and restoration of biodiversity and ecosystems

For an economic activity to be considered Taxonomy-eligible, it must:

1. Contribute substantially to one or more of the environmental objectives
2. Do no significant harm to any of the other environmental objectives
3. Comply with minimum social and governance safeguards. Under the Regulation, these are defined as in alignment with the OECD Guidelines for Multinational Enterprises and UN Guiding Principles on Business and Human Rights, including the International Labour Organisation's ('ILO') declaration on Fundamental Rights and Principles at Work, the eight ILO core conventions and the International Bill of Human Rights.

With this definition, economic activities, even when making a substantial contribution to climate change mitigation and/or adaptation, will not be eligible if they cannot be performed in a way that avoids significant harm to other environmental objectives.

### 7.2.3. Scope/Geography

The "Do no significant harm" criteria recommended by the TEG are often based on existing European environmental law. An example for such criterion would be the acceptable threshold for water contamination for a manufacturing plant, which is found in EU legislation. Therefore, the TEG-recommended criteria are not directly applicable to economic activities located outside the EU. At the same time, many potential users of the EU taxonomy have portfolios with worldwide economic activities. The TEG addressed this issue by pointing to the Technical Screening Criteria that the group considered to be of global relevance. The criteria were flagged as such in the TEG report (p 54) : "*It is the view of the TEG that this criterion is globally relevant. The performance level in the criterion is designed to be consistent with a net zero by 2050 goal. The performance level is not tied specifically to EU regulations, though cross-reference is made where appropriate to those regulations to assist EU users.*"

The TEG recognises that locally relevant standards may reasonably be applied in countries outside the EU. In cases where a locally relevant threshold has been used to assess the environmental performance of an economic activity, the TEG invites companies and investors to provide additional details setting out the rationale for variation from the TEG standard. Those additional details, however, would not make the activity EU Taxonomy-aligned (unless the criteria are equivalent to or more ambitious than the EU threshold).

The TEG also proposed some principles for design of taxonomies by individual countries, in order to foster international taxonomy harmonisation. Taxonomies should specify specific environmental goals. They should cover a list of economic activities, using a classification system. They should use performance metrics, and performance thresholds for each economic activity.

Two bodies will focus on advancing the issue of international applicability and coordination of the EU taxonomy. The first of these two bodies is the International Platform on Sustainable Finance set up by the EC in September 2019. The second is the future Platform on Sustainable Finance set out in the Regulation, to be established in September 2020 to succeed the TEG.

### 7.2.4. Scope/ Sector approach/Use of NACE codes

The TEG decided to use the NACE[2] industrial classification system of economic activities in order to define the EU taxonomy technical screening criteria. While NACE code frameworks are consistent with the vast majority of economic data produced today at EU level[3], and reconcilable with EU national economic and statistical frameworks, there are consequences to using such frameworks. A NACE codes- based taxonomy is not obviously reconcilable with other classification systems widely used by private financial markets participants to analyse their data, such as the GICS (Global Industrial Classification System). Other issues may appear when NACE codes and the notion of "economic activity" are applied for practical purposes. A bond issued by a construction company will be recorded under certain reporting frameworks under the NACE code "construction" of the holding company. However, this bond may be a green bond with use of proceeds for building a solar farm. Furthermore, large corporates often issue their bonds at the level of a holding company recorded under the "finance" NACE code, which is not covered by the presently available version of the EU taxonomy[4]. A consequence could be that the use of NACE codes may not capture all economic activities that are potentially environmentally sustainable. This issue and possible solutions will materialise at the time of implementation of the Regulation.

Another potential issue could be the adequacy of the NACE classification system in the context of mapping of investments to determine Paris Agreement compatibility. The NACE reporting framework is fully consistent with GDP accounting and so suffers the same shortcomings as GDP in its capacity to capture environmental sustainability. These flaws are well documented (Stiglitz, Fitoussi and Durand, 2018[3]). In addition, some new transition activities or sectors such as Carbon Capture and Storage do not exist in NACE. For the purposes of the TEG report, some additions have been made in the report to the existing NACE framework. For example, buildings do not have their own specific NACE code. Natural capital preservation, restoration and creation and related services also do not have NACE codes for the time being. NACE codes were supplemented by additional codes CEPA (Classification of Environmental Protection Activities) (European Commission, 2020[4])and CREMA (Classification of Resource Management Activities) (European Commission, 2020[5]) because of these gaps.

Furthermore, an economic activity cannot be considered sustainable independent of the wider system in which it operates – one of the key themes in OECD work on "accelerating climate action" (OECD, 2019[6]). Critical systems examples are the energy, transport, urban, water and food systems. For example, the environmental sustainability of emissions reductions enabled by an electric vehicle depends on a number of factors, e.g. the carbon-intensity of the electricity used to charge the battery, the extent to which the vehicle adds to traffic congestion, whether there is reuse or recycling at the end of battery life. In order to substantially contribute to environmental objectives, the critical aspects of a system -- i.e. resources used, transformation processes and infrastructure underpinning the system -- must be decarbonised and made resilient. In addition, the nature of the transition in each country or region will be influenced by the evolution of the entire system, including local strategies and policies. A Taxonomy-eligible activity may only contribute to an individual country or region's transition pathway when it is also coherent with the transition of the overall system of which the activity is a part. Wherever possible, the EU Taxonomy criteria have attempted to take a systems approach into account. However, this is necessarily limited in an activity-based approach.

### 7.2.5. Principles

The following principles have guided the development of the draft EU taxonomy:

- Technology neutrality: The selected criteria must not discriminate between technologies, provided they have the same impact on environmental objectives.
- Dynamic and evolving tool: The dynamic character of the transition and the uncertainty related to technology result in a need to update the thresholds, which in some cases are set to decline over time to be consistent with a chosen transition pathway. The EC Platform set up to succeed the TEG in 2020 will be tasked with reviewing and adjusting the criteria as appropriate.
- Easy to understand and use: The purpose of the taxonomy is to be understood and used by financial market participants, so it must be user-friendly, and not too costly for users in terms of expenditures and time.
- Enabling transition activities, versus a "binary" "green or not" approach. The taxonomy scopes three kinds of economic activities:
  - Activities that are already low carbon: i.e. with very low, zero or net negative emissions, and compatible with a net zero CO2 economy by 2050. Examples include renewable energy, zero emissions transport, and afforestation.
  - Activities that contribute to the transition to a net zero economy in 2050. The list of those activities may need to be revised regularly and tightened over time. Examples include building renovation, electricity generation up to 100 gr CO2/kWh, or cars generating less than 50 gr CO2/km.
  - Activities that enable emissions reductions in the first two types of activities above. They are for instance manufacture of wind turbines, or the installation of efficient boilers in building, provided certain criteria are met.

Additional details on these activities are provided below.

## 7.3. Metrics and thresholds

The Annex to this report provides an overview of the proposed criteria for substantial contribution to economic activities that mitigate climate. As stated above, each of those criteria goes with other criteria for "do no significant harm" (DNSH) to climate adaptation and four other environmental objectives posed in the regulation. For the sake of brevity, this overview does not provide details on the DNSH criteria.

## 7.4. Outlook and next steps

### *7.4.1. Coverage of the taxonomy and extension to more economic activities*

The EU Taxonomy aims to have extensive coverage, with 72 economic activities included. Those activities were prioritised according to their contribution to total GHG emissions in the EU in 2017.

Table 7.1. GHG emissions for sectors considered in the TEG taxonomy, EU-28, 2017

| NACE macro-sector | GHG (Tonne) | Share of GHG (% of GHG from all NACE Macro-sectors) |
|---|---|---|
| A- Agriculture, forestry and fishing | 520,860,082.54 | 14.7% |
| B – Mining and quarrying | 79,624,366.67 | 2.3% |
| C- Manufacturing | 846,420,845.95 | 23.9% |
| D- Electricity, gas, steam and air conditioning supply | 1,072,529,498.49 | 30.3% |
| E – Water supply, sewerage, waste management and remediation | 163,285,205.41 | 4.6% |
| F – Construction | 60,058,074.32 | 1.7% |
| H- Transportation and storage | 535,602,112.51 | 15.2% |
| J- Information an communication | 10,396,008.51 | 0.3% |
| L- Real estate activities | 6,246,240.47 | 0.2% |
| Total A-F, H, J, L | 3,295,022,434.87 | 93.2% |

More activities may be added to the taxonomy in the future as implementation starts. Within the sectors already covered, some of the TEG recommendations for activities to be added in the future have been described in Section 3 of this annex.

## 7.5. Future steps mentioned in the taxonomy regulation

The EC will review the taxonomy regulation two years after its entry into force, and then every three years. A "brown taxonomy" could be proposed by the end of 2021, as well as criteria related to social aspects. In its revision of the Taxonomy Regulation, the EC will consider possible effects of the Taxonomy Regulation on stranded assets, costs and benefits of implementation, and impact in terms of increasing sustainable finance flows.

### *7.5.1. Use of the Taxonomy Regulation*

Financial products subject to the NFRD regulation (see below) will need to use the taxonomy when they claim to have an environmentally sustainable investment objective (i.e. financial products referred to under Article 9 in the NFRD). They will need to disclose how and to what extent the taxonomy was used. They will also need to disclose the taxonomy-compliant share of their investment. The same requirements apply to products claiming to have ESG characteristics (referred to under Article 8 of the NFRD). Large corporates subject to the NFRD will need to disclose the taxonomy-compliant share of their turnover, capital expenditures (capex) and operating expenses (opex).

The financial products in scope are:

- Asset Management: UCITS[5] Funds (equity, bond, ETFs[6]), Alternative Investment Funds[7], Portfolio Management.
- Insurance: Insurance Based Insurance Products (IBIPs).

### *7.5.2. Next steps*

*Regarding the Taxonomy Regulation*

The Regulation must be approved formally by an EU Parliament Plenary session during 2020. Delegated Acts must be approved by the end of 2021 for Technical Screening Criteria (TSC) relating to substantial contribution to climate change mitigation and adaptation. TSC relating to substantial contribution on the four other environmental objectives (waste, waste, pollution and ecosystems) will need to be approved by end 2022.

*Regarding other European regulations referencing the Taxonomy Regulation*

The EC signalled its intention to put forward a legislative proposal for a EU Green Bond Standard in 2020. In order to be eligible to the Standard, the use of proceeds of green bonds will need to be aligned with the EU Taxonomy. There would be mandatory verification by accredited verifiers.

# Annex 7.A. Overview of the proposed criteria of the EU Taxonomy

The thresholds and language in this section derive mainly from the final technical report of the TEG, to which readers may refer for the full details. To be more precise, this section attempts to summarise in a condensed way pages 30 to 578 of the Technical Annex to the TEG Final Report on the EU Taxonomy. The focus is on thresholds and metrics, rather than principles or rationales, given the scope of the present report.

## Forestry

The following economic activities are addressed in the Taxonomy: afforestation, reforestation, restoration, rehabilitation, forest management and conservation forest. There are some differences and nuances in the metrics and thresholds between these sub-categories. A broad, indicative summary of them is:

- Continued compliance with Sustainable Forest Management criteria
- Verified GHG balance baseline for above-ground carbon pools
- Above-ground carbon stocks must increase above the baseline

Forestry criteria are considered by the TEG to be of international relevance

## Agriculture

In the EU, 10% of GHG emissions are attributed to agriculture. The following economic activities are addressed in the Taxonomy:

- Growing of non-perennial crops (including cereals, rice, vegetables…)
- Growing of perennial crops (including grapes, fruit, beverage crops…)
- Livestock production: including dairy, other cattle, pigs, poultry…

A broad, indicative summary of applicable criteria is:

- Avoid or reduce GHG emissions, including those from inputs used on the farm, through the application of appropriate management practices
- Maintain and increase existing carbon stocks for a period equal to or greater than 20 years through the application of appropriate management practices
- Land was not deemed previously to be "of high carbon stock", such as peat lands and wetlands.

## Manufacturing

The manufacturing section of the Taxonomy includes both the manufacturing of low-carbon technologies as well as energy-intensive and hard-to-abate manufacturing sectors. Specifically, this includes: the manufacturing of aluminium (NACE 24.42); the manufacturing of iron and steel (NACE 24.1, 24.2, 24.3); the manufacturing of cement (NACE 23.51); and the manufacturing of chemicals (NACE 20.13, 20.14, 20.15, 20.16). It aims to give support to those economic activities that are low in carbon emissions and to first movers who are engaging in a transformational shift.

Additionally, the Taxonomy includes manufacturing activities that produce the products and technologies that can contribute to GHG emissions reductions in other sectors of the economy. Specifically, this refers to the manufacturing of products, key components, equipment and machinery that are essential to a number of key renewable energy technologies (geothermal power, hydropower, concentrated solar power (CSP), solar photovoltaic (PV) technology, wind energy and ocean energy); the manufacturing of low-carbon transport vehicles, fleets and vessels; and the manufacturing of energy efficiency equipment for buildings. The TEG was not able to complete work for other manufacturing sectors, including mining, due to time constraints and the complexity of the issues.

The criteria focus on reducing GHG emissions caused by manufacturing activities up to the levels of performance achieved by best performers. The criteria generally cover both Scope 1 and Scope 2 emissions. The EU ETS benchmarks have been the main reference for setting such thresholds, as they correspond to the level of performance achieved by the 10% best installations in the EU and are updated regularly.

There are no explicit thresholds for those manufacturing activities listed under the category "low carbon technologies". No criteria on the GHG emissions from manufacturing of listed products are specified since the mitigation benefits of these products, components, equipment and technologies are considered to outweigh the emissions generated as a result of the manufacturing process to generate them.

### *Low Carbon Technologies*

This sector includes:

- Manufacture of products, key components and machinery that are essential for eligible renewable energy technologies (associated conversion efficiency requirements are set in the Renewable Energy Directive (2018/2001/EU)).
- Manufacture of low carbon transport vehicles and their respective key components, fleets and vessels meeting specific criteria:
    - For passenger cars, light commercial vehicles ($CO_2$ Regulation for cars and vans (EU) 2019/631):
        - Until 2025: vehicles with tailpipe emission intensity no greater than 50 g $CO_2$/km. This also includes vehicles with zero tailpipe emissions (e.g. electric, hydrogen).
        - From 2026 onwards: only vehicles with emission intensity of 0g $CO_2$/km
    - For category L vehicles (e.g. motorcycles):
        - Zero tailpipe emission vehicles (incl. hydrogen, fuel cell, electric)
    - Heavy-duty vehicles: N2 and N3 vehicles, as defined by the Heavy Duty $CO_2$ Regulation (EU) 2019/1242):
        - Zero direct emission heavy-duty vehicles that emit less than 1g CO2/kWh (or 1g $CO_2$ /km for certain N2 vehicles);
        - Low-emission heavy-duty vehicles with specific direct $CO_2$ emissions of less than 50% of the reference $CO_2$ emissions of all vehicles in the same sub-group.
    - Rail fleets:
        - Zero direct emission trains
    - Urban, suburban and interurban passenger land transport fleets:
        - Zero direct emission land transport fleets (e.g. light rail transit, metro, tram, trolleybus, bus and rail)
    - Water transport:
        - Zero direct emission waterborne vessels

- Manufacture of the following products for energy efficient equipment for buildings and their key components is eligible:
  - Installation of Building Management Systems (BMS)
  - High efficiency windows (U-value better than 0.7 W/m2K)
  - High efficiency doors (U-value better than 1.2 W/m2K)
  - Insulation products with low thermal conductivity (lambda lower or equal to 0.045 W/mK), external cladding with U-value lower than 0.5 W/m2K and roofing systems with U-value lower than 0.3 W/m2K)
  - Hot water fittings (e.g. taps, showers) that are rated in the top class of the European Water Label Scheme (http://www.europeanwaterlabel.eu/)
  - Household appliances (e.g. washing machines, dishwashers) rated in the top available class according to the EU Energy Label for each type of appliance
  - High efficiency lighting appliances rated in the highest energy efficiency class that is significantly populated in the energy efficiency label (or higher classes) according to EU Energy labels
  - Presence and daylight controls for lighting systems

### *Cement*

Thresholds for cement clinker (A) are applicable to plants that produce clinker only, and do not produce finished cement. All other plants need to meet the thresholds for cement (B) or alternative binder.

**(A) Cement clinker**

Specific emissions (calculated according to the methodology used for EU-ETS benchmarks) associated with the clinker production processes must be lower than the value of the related EU-ETS benchmark. As of February 2020, the EU-ETS benchmark value for cement clinker manufacturing is: 0.766 $tCO_2e$/t of clinker[8].

**(B) Cement**

Specific emissions associated with the clinker and cement production processes are lower than 0.498 of $tCO_2e$/t cement or alternative binder.

### *Aluminium*

Manufacture of primary aluminium is eligible if Criteria 1 is met in combination with either Criterion 2 or 3 below.

- Criterion 1: Direct emission for primary aluminium production is at or below the value of the related EU-ETS benchmark. As of February 2020, the EU-ETS benchmark value for aluminium manufacturing is 1.514 tCO2e/t. Direct emissions are to be calculated according to the methodology used for EU-ETS benchmarks.
- Criterion 2: Electricity consumption for electrolysis is at or below 15.29 MWh/t (European average emission factor according to International Aluminium Institute, 2017, to be updated annually)
- Criterion 3: Average carbon intensity of the electricity that is used for primary aluminium production (electrolysis) is at or below 100 g CO2e/kWh (Taxonomy threshold for electricity production, subject to periodic update).

Manufacture of secondary aluminium (i.e. production of aluminium from recycled aluminium) is eligible. No additional mitigation criteria need to be met.

### *Iron and Steel*

Manufacturing of iron and steel is eligible if the GHG emissions (calculated according to the methodology used for EU-ETS benchmarks) associated with the production processes are lower than the values of the related EU-ETS benchmarks. As of February 2020, the EU-ETS benchmarks values for iron and steel manufacturing are:

- Hot metal = 1.328 $tCO_2e$/t product
- Sintered ore = 0.171 $tCO_2e$/t product
- Iron casting = 0.325 $tCO_2e$/t product
- Electric Arc Furnace (EAF) high alloy steel = 0.352 $tCO_2e$/t product
- Electric Arc Furnace (EAF) carbon steel = 0.283 $tCO_2e$/t product
- Coke (excluding lignite coke) = 0.286 $tCO_2e$/t product

All new steel production, or combination of new and recycled steel production, is eligible if the emissions fall below the thresholds above. Additionally, all production of steel in an Electric Arc Furnace where at least 90% of the iron content in the final products is sourced from scrap steel is considered eligible. In this case, no other thresholds are applicable.

### *Manufacture of hydrogen*

The following thresholds need to be met:

- Direct CO2 emissions from manufacturing of hydrogen: 5.8 tCO2e/t Hydrogen in alignment with energy thresholds in the taxonomy.
- Electricity use for hydrogen produced by electrolysis is at or lower than 58 MWh/t Hydrogen.
- Average carbon intensity of the electricity produced and used for hydrogen manufacturing is at or below 100 g CO2e/kWh (Taxonomy threshold for electricity production, subject to periodic update).

### *Other inorganic basic chemicals*

Manufacturing of carbon black and soda ash are eligible if the GHG emissions (calculated according to the methodology used for EU-ETS benchmarks) associated with the production processes are lower than the values of the related EU-ETS benchmarks. As of February 2020, the EU-ETS benchmarks values are:

- Carbon black: 1.954 $tCO_2e$/t
- Soda ash: 0.843 $tCO_2e$/t

Manufacturing of chlorine is eligible if the two following thresholds are met:

- Electricity use for chlorine manufacturing is at or lower than 2.45 MWh/t chlorine (includes both electrolysis and chlorine treatment, threshold subject to periodic update)
- Average carbon intensity of the electricity that is used for chlorine manufacturing is at or below 100 g $CO_2e$/kWh (Taxonomy threshold for electricity production, subject to periodic update).

### *Other organic basic chemicals:*

This activity comprises the manufacturing of high value chemicals, aromatics, ethylene chloride, vinyl chloride, ethylbenzene, styrene, ethylene oxide, monoethylene glycol and adipic acid. It also comprises organic chemicals falling under the following Eurostat Classification of Products by Activity (CPA) codes:

- Saturated acyclic monocarboxylic acids and their derivatives (CPA code 20.14.32)

- Unsaturated monocarboxylic, cyclanic, cyclenic or cycloterpenic acyclic polycarboxylic acids and their derivatives (CPA code 20.14.33)
- Aromatic polycarboxylic and carboxylic acids with additional oxygen functions; and their derivatives, except salicylic acid and its salts (CPA code 20.14.34)

For the manufacturing of all chemicals covered in this activity (except the manufacture of the following CPA product categories: 20.14.32, 20.14.33, 20.14.34), the selected metric is GHG emissions per unit of production ($tCO_2e/t$) (emissions factor). GHG emissions must be calculated according to the methodology used for EU-ETS benchmarks. ETS product benchmarks only for the manufacturing of all chemicals covered in this activity (except the manufacturing of the following CPA product categories: 20.14.32, 20.14.33, 20.14.34):

- For HVC: 0,702 tCO2e/t
- For aromatics: 0,0295 tCO2e/t t216
- For vinyl chloride: 0,204 tCO2e/t
- For styrene: 0,527 tCO2e/t
- For ethylene oxide/ethylene glycols: 0,512 tCO2e/t

### *Fertilizers and nitrogen compounds*

This activity comprises the manufacturing of nitric acid and anhydrous ammonia.

- Manufacturing of nitric acid is eligible if the GHG emissions (calculated according to the methodology used for EU-ETS benchmarks) associated with the production processes are lower than the values of the related EU-ETS benchmarks. As of February 2020, the EU-ETS benchmarks values for the manufacturing of nitric acid are 0.302 tCO2e/t.
- Manufacturing of ammonia is eligible if the two following thresholds are met:
  - Scope 1 emissions lower than 1 $tCO_2/t$ Ammonia, and
  - Combined $CO_2$ emissions (Scope 1 emissions and Scope 2 emissions, from electricity consumed) lower than 1.3 $tCO_2/t$ Ammonia.
  - For the calculation of the emissions from the manufacturing process of Ammonia, both steps are considered: production of the intermediate product hydrogen and synthesis of the Ammonia. Scope 1 emissions encompass emissions from both steps.

### *Manufacture of plastics in primary form*

Manufacture of plastics in primary form shall comply with at least one of the following three criteria, with additional criteria applying in specific cases (see below).

- The plastics in primary form are manufactured by mechanical recycling
- The plastics in primary form are manufactured by chemical recycling including: chemical depolymerisation (aka monomerisation), pyrolysis, gasification, solvent-based purification of polymers. When this criterion is applied, the carbon footprint of the plastics in primary form, manufactured by chemical recycling (excluding any calculated benefit from the production of fuels), shall be lower than the carbon footprint of the plastics in primary form manufactured with fossil fuel feedstock. The carbon footprint shall be calculated in accordance with ISO 14067:2018 and validated by a third party.
- Manufacture of plastics in primary form shall be wholly or partially derived from renewable feedstock and the carbon footprint of the plastics in primary form, manufactured wholly or partially from renewable feedstock shall be lower than the carbon footprint of the plastics in primary form

manufactured with fossil fuel feedstock. The carbon footprint shall be calculated in accordance with ISO 14067:2018 and validated by a third party. For the purpose of applying this criterion, renewable feedstock refers to biomass, industrial bio-waste or municipal bio-waste. Additional criteria apply in the case of renewable feedstock.

- In addition to the three criteria above, an independent sector study must confirm that at least 90% of the type of plastic manufactured is: (1) not used for single use consumer products, or (2) based on recycled plastics as feedstock.

## Electricity, gas, steam, and air conditioning supply

Heat and electricity generation are responsible for over a quarter of the EU's greenhouse gas emissions (Eurostat, 2016[7]). Technology-agnostic criteria have been developed for different sources of electricity and heating and cooling. The criteria account for the important role in meeting the EU's net-zero emissions objective of improvements to the supporting infrastructure associated with delivering both types of energy. The TEG has developed these Taxonomy criteria for the energy sector so they can be used globally.

An overarching, technology-agnostic emissions intensity threshold of 100g $CO_2e$ /kWh is proposed for electricity generation, heat production and the co-generation of heat and electricity. The calculation of the 100g CO2e / kWh threshold is based on the targets for future allowed emissions from the power sector in the EU, divided by the expected evolution of electricity demand[9]. This threshold will be reduced every five years in line with governmental targets set out to achieve net-zero emissions by 2050. For electricity and heat generation activities, an ISO 14067 or a GHG Protocol Product Lifecycle Standard compliant Product Carbon Footprint (PCF) assessment including measurement of fugitive emissions is required. This includes actual physical measurements of methane leakage from the point of extraction/well-head to production of energy (electricity and/or heat). The TEG acknowledged that improved standards and methodologies will develop and recommended that the acceptance of the ISO 14067, GHG Protocol Product Lifecycle Standard and the PCF methodologies be reviewed periodically by the Platform on Sustainable Finance. To aid the transition to a net-zero economy, certain technologies, such as solar, wind and tidal energy received a derogation from the requirement to conduct PCF's assessments on the basis that these technologies currently perform significantly below the emissions intensity threshold. These derogations are subject to regular review in accordance with the declining threshold. Furthermore, in the case where Carbon Capture and Storage (CCS) technologies are used to meet the emissions intensity threshold, a contractual agreement is required as proof to show that the carbon will be transported and sequestered in economic activities which are themselves eligible under the Taxonomy.

The threshold was determined as follows:

- Historical power sector emissions and electricity demand data for EU28 are sourced from Eurostat.
- Future emissions are in line with EU political commitments for the ETS sector (- 43% by 2030), then decline linearly to zero by 2050. Future electricity demand (net generation) is assumed to grow as per the EU 2016 PRIMES Reference Scenario.

These criteria imply that:

- Unabated natural-gas fired power generation is not expected to meet the required threshold. Gas-fired power with carbon capture and sequestration may qualify.
- Blended gas-fired power: Co-combustion of multiple gases for the production of electricity, heat/cool and co-generation is also subject to the emissions intensity threshold. This includes combustion of RED II gases.
- Hydropower: the embedded emissions associated with the construction of hydropower facilities and the alteration of landscapes constitute a significant portion of lifecycle analysis emissions. Such emissions can be compensated for, by a complementary emissions reduction activity.

The experts identified further economic activities that could be relevant for the Taxonomy. However, these activities could not be assessed in detail by the TEG and were left to future consideration by the Platform on Sustainable Finance. Such economic activities may include:

- The ownership, operation and recycling of energy storage facilities.
- Other gas infrastructure, except pipelines, which are relevant to the switch to hydrogen and zero-carbon gases and the recycling of existing gas infrastructure.
- CCU applications, which ensure CO2 retention,
- Other eligible energy (electricity, co-generation, heat/cool) assets that can be included, such as production of heat/cool from ocean energy.

### *Production of electricity from photovoltaic solar system (solar PV)*

Any electricity generation technology can be included in the Taxonomy if it can be demonstrated, using an ISO 14067 or a GHG Protocol Product Lifecycle Standard-compliant Product Carbon Footprint (PCF) assessment, that the life cycle impacts for producing 1 kWh of electricity are below the declining threshold.

- Declining threshold: Facilities operating at life cycle emissions lower than 100g $CO_2$e/kWh, declining to net-0g $CO_2$e/kWh by 2050, are eligible.
- This threshold will be reduced every 5 years in line with a net-zero $CO_2$e in 2050 trajectory.
- Assets and activities must meet the threshold at the point in time when taxonomy approval is sought.
- For activities that operate beyond 2050, it must be technically feasible to reach net-zero emissions in Scope 1 emissions.

However:

- Solar PV is currently derogated from performing a PCF or GHG lifecycle assessment subject to regular review in accordance with the declining threshold.
- Solar PV is currently deemed to be Taxonomy eligible; this decision is subject to regular review.

### *Production of electricity from concentrated solar power (CSP)*

The same contents as in paragraph 51 above applies. For activities which operate beyond 2050, it must be technically feasible to reach net-zero emissions.

However:

- CSP is currently derogated from performing a PCF or GHG lifecycle assessment subject to regular review in accordance with the declining threshold.
- CSP is currently deemed to be Taxonomy eligible; this decision is subject to regular review.
- Cogeneration of Heat and Power is covered under Construction and operation of a facility used for cogeneration of heat/cooling and Power threshold. Generation of heat/cool is covered under the Generation of heat/cool threshold.

### *Production of electricity from wind power*

Any electricity generation technology can be included in the taxonomy if it can be demonstrated, using an ISO 14067 or a GHG Protocol Product Lifecycle Standard-compliant Product Carbon Footprint (PCF) assessment, that the life cycle impacts for producing 1 kWh of electricity are below the declining threshold.

- Declining threshold: Facilities operating at life cycle emissions lower than 100g CO2e/kWh, declining to net-0g CO2e/kWh by 2050, are eligible.

- This threshold will be reduced every 5 years in line with a net-zero CO2e in 2050 trajectory.
- Assets and activities must meet the threshold at the point in time when taxonomy approval is sought.
- For activities which operate beyond 2050, it must be technically feasible to reach net-zero emissions.

However:

- Wind power is currently derogated from performing a PCF or GHG lifecycle assessment subject to regular review in accordance with the declining threshold.
- Wind power is currently deemed to be Taxonomy eligible, which is subject to regular review.

### *Production of electricity from ocean energy*

Any electricity generation technology can be included in the taxonomy if it can be demonstrated, using an ISO 14067 or a GHG Protocol Product Lifecycle Standard-compliant Product Carbon Footprint (PCF) assessment, that the life cycle impacts for producing 1 kWh of electricity are below the declining threshold.

- Declining threshold: Facilities operating at life cycle emissions lower than 100g $CO_2e$/kWh, declining to net-0g $CO_2e$/kWh by 2050, are eligible.
- This threshold will be reduced every 5 years in line with a net-zero $CO_2e$ in 2050 trajectory.
- Assets and activities must meet the threshold at the point in time when taxonomy approval is sought.
- For activities which operate beyond 2050, it must be technically feasible to reach net-zero emissions.

However:

- Ocean energy is currently derogated from performing a PCF or GHG lifecycle assessment subject to regular review in accordance with the declining threshold.
- Ocean energy is currently deemed to be Taxonomy eligible, which is subject to regular review.
- Combined Heat and Power is covered under Construction and operation of a facility used for cogeneration of heat/cooling and Power threshold

### *Production of electricity from hydropower*

Any electricity generation technology can be included in the taxonomy if it can be demonstrated, using an ISO 14067 or a GHG Protocol Product Lifecycle Standard-compliant Product Carbon Footprint (PCF) assessment, that the life cycle impacts for producing 1 kWh of electricity are below the declining threshold. Hydropower facilities with a power density above 5 W/m2 are currently derogated from conducting the PCF or GHG Lifecycle Assessment (subject to regular review in accordance with the declining threshold)[10]. As part of the ISO 14067 G-res tool[11] and the IEA Hydro Framework[12] are acceptable methodologies. Allocated emissions should be calculated according to the operating regime, as per the allocation methodology developed by UNESCO/IHA and embedded in the G-res tool and IEA Hydro Framework. These criteria also apply to pumped-storage facilities.

The full PCF assessment shall be subject to review.

- Declining threshold: Facilities operating at life cycle emissions lower than 100g $CO_2e$/kWh, declining to net-0g $CO_2e$/kWh by 2050, are eligible.
  - This threshold will be reduced every 5 years in line with a net-zero $CO_2e$ in 2050 trajectory.

- Assets and activities must meet the threshold at the point in time when taxonomy approval is sought.
- For activities which operate beyond 2050, it must be technically feasible to reach net-zero emissions.

### *Production of electricity from geothermal sector*

Any electricity generation technology can be included in the taxonomy if it can be demonstrated, using an ISO 14067 or a GHG Protocol Product Lifecycle Standard-compliant Product Carbon Footprint (PCF) assessment, that the life cycle impacts for producing 1 kWh of electricity are below the declining threshold[13]. A full PCF or GHG lifecycle assessment shall be applied, using project specific-data where relevant, and shall be subject to review.

- Declining threshold: Facilities operating at life cycle emissions lower than 100g $CO_2$e/kWh, declining to net-0g $CO_2$e/kWh by 2050, are eligible.
- This threshold will be reduced every 5 years in line with a net-zero $CO_2$e in 2050 trajectory.
- Assets and activities must meet the threshold at the point in time when taxonomy approval is sought.
- For activities which operate beyond 2050, it must be technically feasible to reach net-zero emissions.
- Combined Heat and Power is covered under Construction and operation of a facility used for cogeneration of heat/cooling and Power threshold

### *Production of electricity from gas (not exclusive to natural gas)*

Any electricity generation technology can be included in the taxonomy if it can be demonstrated, using an ISO 14067 or a GHG Protocol Product Lifecycle Standard-compliant Product Carbon Footprint (PCF) assessment, that the life cycle impacts for producing 1 kWh of electricity are below the declining threshold. A full PCF shall be applied, using project specific data where relevant and shall be subject to review. This assessment should include actual physical measurements, i.e. methane leakage measurements across gas extraction, transport and storage systems.

- Declining threshold: Facilities operating at life cycle emissions lower than 100g $CO_2$e/kWh, declining to net-0g $CO_2$e/kWh by 2050, are eligible.
- This threshold will be reduced every 5 years in line with a net-zero $CO_2$e in 2050 trajectory.
- Assets and activities must meet the threshold at the point in time when taxonomy approval is sought.
- For activities which operate beyond 2050, it must be technically feasible to reach net-zero emissions.
- Facilities that will incorporate any form of abatement (e.g. CCS, Co-firing, other…) must show that the abatement activity is eligible under the Taxonomy.
- Electricity generation from other fossil-fuel based gases would be eligible under the Taxonomy, subject to meeting the declining emissions threshold.
- Combined Heat and Power is covered under Construction and operation of a facility used for cogeneration of heat/cooling and Power threshold.

### *Production of electricity from bioenergy (biomass, biogas and biofuels)*

Production of electricity from biofuels shall be assessed in relation to the relative fossil fuel comparator set out in RED II. Facilities operating above 80% of GHG emissions-reduction in relation to the relative fossil fuel comparator set out in RED II increasing to 100% by 2050, are eligible. Facilities must use feedstocks which meet the criteria on the manufacture of biomass, biogas and biofuels.

- This threshold will be reduced every 5 years in line with a net-zero $CO_2e$ in 2050 trajectory.
- Assets and activities must meet the threshold at the point in time when taxonomy approval is sought.
- For activities that go beyond 2050, it must be technically feasible to reach net-zero emissions.
- For anaerobic digestion of biowaste and sewage sludge, reference is made to relevant Taxonomy activities. Any other anaerobic digestion of organic material is eligible provided that:

methane leakage from relevant facilities (e.g. for biogas production and storage, energy generation, digestate storage) is controlled by a monitoring plan.

the digestate produced is used as fertiliser/soil improver, directly or after composting or any other treatment.

### *Transmission and distribution of electricity*

All electricity transmission and distribution infrastructure or equipment in systems that are on a trajectory to full decarbonisation (see below) are eligible, except for infrastructure that:

- Is dedicated to creating a direct connection, or expanding an existing direct connection between a power production plant that is more $CO_2$ intensive than 100 g $CO_2e$/kWh, measured on a Levelised Cost of Electricity (LCE) basis, and a substation or network.
- A system[14] is deemed to be on a trajectory to full decarbonisation if either
  - more than 67% of newly connected generation capacity in the system is below the generation threshold value of 100 g $CO_2e$/kWh measured on a PCF basis, over a rolling five-year period; or
  - the average system grid emissions factor is below the threshold value of 100 g CO2e/kWh measured on a PCF basis, over a rolling five-year average period. These criteria will be subject to regular review, in line with reviews of generation threshold values and progress to decarbonisation.
  - Based on the results of an assessment carried out in 2019 by the EU Joint Research Centre (JRC), the interconnected European system meets the criteria above that define a system to be on a trajectory to full decarbonisation. It, and its subordinated systems, meet the eligibility criteria for this activity and are derogated from carrying out the quantitative assessment. This derogation will also be subject to regular review, in line with review of the criteria above, or in case of major policy changes that would negatively affect commitments to decarbonisation.
- The following transmission and distribution (T&D) grid related activities are eligible, irrespective of whether the system is on a pathway to full decarbonisation:
  - Direct connection, or expansion of existing direct connection, of low carbon electricity generation below the threshold of 100 g CO2e/kWh declining to 0 g CO2e/kWh in 2050, measured on a PCF basis, to a substation or network.
  - Electric vehicle charging stations and supporting electric infrastructure for the electrification of transport, subject to Taxonomy eligibility under the transport section.
  - Installation of T&D transformers that comply with the Tier 2 (2021) requirements from Regulation 548/2014 on the eco-design of small, medium and large power transformers and, for medium power transformers with highest voltage for equipment not exceeding 36 kV, with AAA0 level requirements on no-load losses set out in standard EN 50588-1.

- Equipment and infrastructure where the main objective is an increase of the generation or use of renewable electricity generation
- Equipment to increase the controllability and observability of the electricity system and enable the development and integration of renewable energy sources (details are provided)
- Equipment to carry information to users for remotely acting on consumption
- Equipment to allow for exchange of renewable electricity between users

Interconnectors between transmission systems are eligible, provided that one of the systems is eligible.

### *Storage of electricity*

This activity includes the construction and operation of facilities that store electricity and return it at a later time, in the form of electricity. Currently all electricity storage activities are eligible under the Taxonomy, subject to regular review. Eligibility criteria for demand side management (load shedding and load shifting) activities are available under the transmission & distribution of electricity criteria. However, hydropower pumped storage shall comply with the criteria for "production of electricity from hydropower".

### *Storage of thermal energy*

This activity includes the construction and operation of facilities that store thermal energy, and return it at a later time, in the form of thermal energy or other energy vectors. Currently all thermal energy storage is eligible under the Taxonomy (including thermal energy storage (UTES) or aquifer thermal energy storage (ATES)), subject to regular review.

### *Storage of hydrogen*

This activity includes the construction and operation of facilities that store hydrogen, and return it at a later time, in the form of hydrogen or other energy vectors. Currently construction of hydrogen storage assets is eligible under the Taxonomy, subject to regular review. Operation of hydrogen storage assets is eligible under the Taxonomy if the infrastructure is used to store Taxonomy-eligible hydrogen (see manufacture of hydrogen). Infrastructure that is required for zero direct emissions transport (e.g. hydrogen fuelling stations) is eligible under the transport section.

### *Manufacture of biomass, biogas or biofuels*

The manufacture of biomass, biogas and biofuels is eligible if produced from the advanced feedstock listed in Part A of Annex IX of Directive (EU) 2018/2001. For anaerobic digestion of biowaste and sewage sludge, refer to the corresponding Taxonomy activities. Any other anaerobic digestion of organic material is eligible provided that:

- methane leakage from relevant facilities (e.g. for biogas production and storage, energy generation, digestate storage) is controlled by a monitoring plan;
- the digestate produced is used as fertiliser/soil improver, directly or after composting or any other treatment.

### *Retrofit of gas transmission and distribution networks*

The complete system must have been in place and operating for a minimum of 5 years.

- Retrofit of gas transmission and distribution networks whose main purpose is the integration of hydrogen and other low-carbon gases is eligible.

- Any gas transmission or distribution network activities which enable the network to increase the blend of hydrogen and/or other low carbon gasses in the gas system is eligible
- The repair of existing gas pipelines for the reduction of methane leakage is eligible if the pipelines are hydrogen-ready and/or other low carbon gasses-ready.
- Retrofit of gas networks whose main purpose is the integration of captured $CO_2$ is eligible, if the operation of the pipeline meets the criteria outlined for the transportation of captured $CO_2$. Gas network expansion is not eligible.

### *District heating/cooling distribution*

Construction and operation of pipelines and associated infrastructure for distributing heating and cooling is currently eligible, if the system meets the definition of efficient district heat/cool systems in the EU Energy Efficiency Directive. The EU Energy Efficiency Directive defines "efficient district heating and cooling" as a district heating or cooling system using at least 50% renewable energy or 50% waste heat or 75% cogenerated heat or 50% of a combination of such energy and heat. The following activities are always eligible:

- Modifications to lower temperature regimes
- Advanced pilot systems (control and energy management systems, internet of things).

### *Installation and operation of electric heat pumps*

Currently, installation and operation of electric heat pumps is eligible (subject to regular review) under the following conditions:

- Refrigerant threshold: Global Warming Potential≤ 675; and
- equipment meets energy efficiency requirements stipulated in the implementing regulations under the Ecodesign Framework Directive[15]

### *Cogeneration of heat/cool and power from concentrated solar power*

Any cogeneration technology can be included in the taxonomy if it can be demonstrated, the same conditions as in paragraph 51 above. However:

- Concentrated solar power is currently derogated from performing a PCF assessment, subject to regular review in accordance with the declining threshold.
- Concentrated solar power is currently deemed to be Taxonomy eligible, which is subject to regular review.
- Generation of heat/cool is covered under the generation of heat/cool threshold

### *Cogeneration of heat/cool and power from geothermal energy*

Any cogeneration technology can be included in the Taxonomy under the same conditions as in paragraph 51 above. In addition, the full PCF assessment shall be subject to review.

### *Cogeneration of heat/cool and power from gas (not exclusive to natural gas)*

Any cogeneration technology can be included in the Taxonomy if it can be demonstrated, using an ISO 14067 or a GHG Protocol Product Lifecycle Standard-compliant Product Carbon Footprint (PCF) assessment, that the life cycle impacts for producing 1 kWh of heat/cool and power are below the declining threshold. A full PCF shall be applied, using project specific data where relevant and shall be subject to review. This assessment should include actual physical measurements, i.e. methane leakage measurements across gas extraction, transport and storage systems.

- Declining threshold: The cogeneration threshold is the combined heat/cool and power threshold of 100 g $CO_2e$/kWh.
- This threshold will be reduced every 5 years in line with a net-zero $CO_2e$ in 2050 trajectory
- Assets and activities must meet the threshold at the point in time when Taxonomy approval is sought
- For activities which go beyond 2050, it must be technically feasible to reach net-zero emissions
- Facilities that will incorporate any form of abatement (e.g. CCS, Co-firing, other…) must show that the abatement activity is eligible under the Taxonomy
- The full PCF assessment shall be subject to review. Cogeneration from other fossil-fuel based gases would be eligible under the Taxonomy, subject to meeting the declining emissions threshold.

### *Cogeneration of heat/cool and power from bioenergy (biomass, biogas, biofuels)*

Facilities operating above 80% of GHG emissions-reduction in relation to the relative fossil fuel comparator set out in Renewable Energy Directive II (RED II) increasing to 100% by 2050 are eligible. Facilities must use feedstocks which meet the criteria on the manufacture of biomass, biogas and biofuels.

- This threshold will be reduced every 5 years in line with a net-zero $CO_2e$ in 2050 trajectory.
- Assets and activities must meet the threshold at the point in time when taxonomy approval is sought.
- For activities which go beyond 2050, it must be technically feasible to reach net-zero emissions.
- For anaerobic digestion of biowaste and sewage sludge, reference is made to the relevant Taxonomy activities. Any other anaerobic digestion of organic material is eligible provided that methane leakage from relevant facilities (e.g. for biogas production and storage, energy generation, digestate storage) is controlled by a monitoring plan; and the digestate produced is used as fertiliser/soil improver, directly or after composting or any other treatment

### *Production of heat/cool from concentrated solar power sector*

Any heat/cool generation technology can be included in the Taxonomy if it can be demonstrated, using an ISO 14067 or a GHG Protocol Product Lifecycle Standard-compliant Product Carbon Footprint (PCF) assessment, that the life cycle impacts for producing 1 kWh of heat/cool are below the declining threshold.

- Declining threshold: Facilities operating at less than 100 g $CO_2e$/kWh, declining to 0g $CO_2e$ /kWh by 2050, are eligible
- This threshold will be reduced every 5 years in line with a net-zero $CO_2e$ in 2050 trajectory
- Assets and activities must meet the threshold at the point in time when Taxonomy approval is sought
- For activities which go beyond 2050, it must be technically feasible to reach net-zero emissions.

However:

- Concentrated solar power is currently derogated from performing a PCF assessment, subject to regular review in accordance with the declining threshold.
- Concentrated solar power is currently deemed to be Taxonomy eligible, which is subject to regular review.

### *Production of heat/cool from geothermal*

Any heat/cool generation technology can be included in the Taxonomy if it can be demonstrated, using an ISO 14067 or a GHG Protocol Product Lifecycle Standard-compliant Product Carbon Footprint (PCF) assessment, that the life cycle impacts for producing 1 kWh of heat/cool are below the declining threshold.

- Declining threshold: Facilities operating at less than 100 g $CO_2$e/kWh, declining to 0g $CO_2$e /kWh by 2050, are eligible
- This threshold will be reduced every 5 years in line with a net-zero $CO_2$e in 2050 trajectory
- Assets and activities must meet the threshold at the point in time when Taxonomy approval is sought
- For activities which go beyond 2050, it must be technically feasible to reach net-zero emissions
- Cogeneration of heat and power is covered under the construction and operation of a facility used for cogeneration of heat/cooling and power threshold.

### *Production of heat/cool from gas combustion*

Any heat/cool generation technology can be included in the Taxonomy if it can be demonstrated, using an ISO 14067 or a GHG Protocol Product Lifecycle Standard-compliant Product Carbon Footprint (PCF) assessment, that the life cycle impacts for producing 1 kWh of heat/cool and power are below the declining threshold. A full PCF shall be applied, using project specific data where relevant and shall be subject to review. This assessment should include actual physical measurements, i.e. methane leakage measurements across gas extraction, transport and storage systems.

- Declining threshold: The cogeneration threshold is the combined heat/cool and power threshold of 100 g $CO_2$e/kWh.
- This threshold will be reduced every 5 years in line with a net-zero $CO_2$e in 2050 trajectory
- Assets and activities must meet the threshold at the point in time when Taxonomy approval is sought
- For activities which go beyond 2050, it must be technically feasible to reach net-zero emissions
- Facilities that will incorporate any form of abatement (e.g. CCS, co-firing, other...) must show that the abatement activity is eligible under the Taxonomy
- The full PCF assessment shall be subject to review. Heat/cool generation from other fossil-fuel based gases would be eligible under the Taxonomy, subject to meeting the declining emissions threshold.

### *Production of heat/cool from bioenergy (biomass, biogas and biofuels)*

Facilities operating above 80% of GHG emissions-reduction in relation to the relative fossil fuel comparator set out in RED II increasing to 100% by 2050, are eligible. Facilities must use feedstocks which meet the criteria on the manufacture of biomass, biogas and biofuels.

- This threshold will be reduced every 5 years in line with a net-zero $CO_2$e in 2050 trajectory
- Assets and activities must meet the threshold at the point in time when Taxonomy approval is sought
- For activities which go beyond 2050, it must be technically feasible to reach net-zero emissions
- For anaerobic digestion of biowaste and sewage sludge, reference is made to relevant Taxonomy activities. Any other anaerobic digestion of organic material is eligible provided that methane leakage from relevant facilities (e.g. for biogas production and storage, energy generation,

digestate storage) is controlled by a monitoring plan, and the digestate produced is used as fertiliser/soil improver, directly or after composting or any other treatment.

### *Production of heat/cool using waste heat*

All recovery of waste heat is eligible.

## Water, sewerage, waste and remediation (including carbon capture and storage)

These sectors are covered by NACE-Codes E36 to E39. They contribute to a rather small share of the EU's total greenhouse gas emissions – water with a 0.2% share and sewerage, waste, remediation with a 4.4% share in 2016. However, advanced solid waste management has the potential to trigger greenhouse gas emission reductions in other sectors of the economy through waste prevention, separate waste collection, waste reuse and recycling. Regarding waste incineration with energy recovery (waste-to-energy, WtE), the opinions of experts consulted by the TEG differed on whether this would be an appropriate environmentally sustainable activity offering a substantial contribution to climate mitigation. According to the political agreement on the Taxonomy Regulation, any activity leading to a significant increase in the incineration of waste (including WtE) is not considered an eligible activity. With the exception of the incineration of non-recyclable hazardous waste, waste incineration is deemed to cause harm to the environmental objectives of the circular economy as per Article 12(d) of the EU Taxonomy Regulation. Therefore, the TEG has not included WtE, but recommends bringing this matter for further discussion and consideration to the Platform on Sustainable Finance.

An important characteristic of the water, sewerage, waste and remediation sectors is that for the identified activities, the climate mitigation effect is an inherent result of key characteristic of the corresponding business model. For example, the energetic utilization of biogas produced through the anaerobic digestion of sewage sludge and bio-waste, or the material recovery from waste for reuse or recycling in other sectors. Hence, the choice of climate mitigation criteria mainly focused on qualitative metrics that seek to secure the execution of the activities/businesses themselves. Only in water collection, treatment and supply, the climate mitigation effect is the result of a more efficient design of the production process (e.g. by raising pump efficiency or reducing leakages). Consequently, concrete quantitative thresholds were defined.

Carbon capture and sequestration (CCS) was included in the Taxonomy because it is a key technology for the decarbonisation of the European Union (EU). It is included in all pathways presented by the European Commission in its Long-Term Strategic Vision document. $CO_2$ transport and storage are established and proven processes, with decades of operation and well-established regulation in the EU. CCS can be eligible in any sector/activity if it enables that primary activity to operate in compliance with the threshold - for example, steel, cement or electricity production. Whilst some $CO_2$ capture technologies can incur an 'energy penalty' of 10-15%, others do not. For example, the Allam cycle[16] being developed by the Net Power Company for natural gas combustion for power generation does not incur an energy penalty, as supercritical $CO_2$ is integrated fully into the power cycle as a coolant. This significantly reduces both energy and water demand. The TEG therefore warned against considering that CCS is a highly energy-intensive technology. The EU has provided clear and extensive assessment and monitoring requirements through the 2009 $CO_2$ Storage Directive. $CO_2$ has already been safely stored in geological formations in Europe for over 20 years.

### *Water collection, treatment and supply*

The front-to-end water collection, treatment and supply system is eligible provided that its performance in terms of energy consumption per cubic meter of final water supply is high or substantially improved. Eligibility is demonstrated by adherence to one of two optional thresholds:

- Option 1: The front-to-end water supply system has a high degree of energy efficiency characterized by an average energy consumption of the system (including abstraction, treatment and distribution) of 0.5 kw/h per cubic meter billed/unbilled authorized water supply or less[17].
- Option 2: The energy efficiency of the front-to-end water supply system is increased substantially:
  - By decreasing the average energy consumption of the system by at least 20% (including abstraction, treatment and distribution; measured in kwh per cubic meter billed/unbilled authorized water supply);
  - Or by closing the gap between the actual leakage of the water supply network and a given target value of low leakage by at least 20%. The unit of measurement is the Infrastructure Leakage Index (ILI)18; the target value of low leakage is an ILI of 1.5.

### *Centralized wastewater treatment*

Construction or extension of centralized wastewater systems including collection (sewer network) and treatment is eligible, provided that the new wastewater treatment acts as a substitute to more GHG emission intensive wastewater treatment systems (such as pit latrines, septic tanks, anaerobic lagoons etc.). No threshold applies.

### *Anaerobic digestion of sewage sludge*

Anaerobic digestion of sewage sludge treatment is eligible provided that:

- Methane leakage from relevant facilities (e.g. for biogas production and storage, energy generation, digestate storage) is controlled by a monitoring plan; and,
- The produced biogas is used directly for the generation of electricity and/or heat, or upgraded to bio-methane for injection in the natural gas grid, or used as vehicle fuel (e.g. as bio CNG) or as feedstock in chemical industry (e.g. for production of $H_2$ and $NH_3$). No threshold applies.

### *Separate collection and transport of non-hazardous waste in source segregated fractions*

- Separate collection and transport of non-hazardous waste is eligible provided that source segregated waste (in single or co-mingled fractions) is separately collected with the aim of preparing for reuse and/or recycling. No threshold applies.

### *Anaerobic digestion of bio-waste*

Anaerobic digestion of bio-waste is eligible provided that:

- The bio-waste is source segregated and collected separately;
- Methane leakage from relevant facilities (e.g. for biogas production and storage, energy generation, digestate storage) is controlled by a monitoring plan;
- The produced biogas is used directly for the generation of electricity and/or heat, or upgraded to bio-methane for injection in the natural gas grid, or used as vehicle fuel (e.g. as bio CNG) or as feedstock in chemical industry (e.g. for production of $H_2$ and $NH_3$);
- The digestate produced is used as fertiliser/soil improver, directly or after composting or any other treatment; and,
- In dedicated bio-waste treatment plants, bio-waste shall constitute a major share of the input feedstock (at least 70%, measured in weight, as an annual average). Co-digestion is eligible only with a minor share (up to 30% of the input feedstock) of advanced bioenergy feedstock listed in

Annex IX of Directive (EU) 2018/2001. If energy crop feedstock covered by Annex IX is used (with a minor share up to 30%) it shall be produced according to criteria defined for Taxonomy Activities "Growing of perennial crops" or "Growing of non-perennial crops" and respect any additional national limitations established for the purpose of biogas production.

### *Composting of bio-waste*

Composting of bio-waste is eligible provided that:

- The bio-waste is source segregated and collected separately;
- Anaerobic digestion is not a technically and economically viable alternative; and,
- The compost produced is used as fertiliser/soil improver[19]. No threshold applies.

### *Material recovery from non-hazardous waste*

Material recovery from separately collected non-hazardous waste is eligible provided that:

- It produces secondary raw materials suitable for substitution of virgin materials in production processes; and
- At least 50%, in terms of weight, of the processed separately collected non-hazardous waste is converted into secondary raw materials.

### *Landfill gas capture and utilization*

Collection and utilization of landfill gas is eligible provided that:

- The landfill has not been opened after the date of entry into force of the Taxonomy;
- The landfill (or landfill cell) where the system is newly installed (or extended and/or retrofitted) is permanently closed and is not taking further waste;
- The produced landfill gas is used directly for the generation of electricity and/or heat, or upgraded to bio-methane for injection in the natural gas grid, or used as vehicle fuel (e.g. as bio CNG) or as feedstock in chemical industry (e.g. for production of H2 and NH3); and,
- Methane emissions from the landfill and leakages from the landfill gas collection and utilization facilities are controlled by a monitoring plan. No threshold applies.

### *Direct Air Capture of $CO_2$*

All activities pertaining to the direct capture of $CO_2$ from the atmosphere to lower global atmospheric $CO_2$ concentration levels are currently eligible, subject to regular review.

### *Capture of Anthropogenic Emissions*

Capture of anthropogenic emissions is currently eligible provided that:

- It enables the economic activity to operate under its respective threshold; and,
- It demonstrates that the captured $CO_2$ will be offloaded to a Taxonomy eligible $CO_2$ transportation operation and permanent sequestration facility. This criterion is subject to regular review.

### *Transport of $CO_2$*

Transport modalities that contribute to the transport of $CO_2$ to eligible permanent sequestration sites are eligible, only if the asset operates below the leakage/tonne of $CO_2$ threshold. Leakage/tonne of $CO_2$

transported from head(s) of the carbon dioxide transport network to injection point(s) must be <0.5%. The $CO_2$ must be delivered to a Taxonomy-eligible permanent sequestration site or to other transport modalities which lead directly to an eligible permanent sequestration site. For assets or activities that enable carbon capture and use (CCU), any and all of the connected elements of an existing transport network are ineligible. Assets which increase the flexibility and management of an existing network, without expanding the network to include carbon capture and use activities, are eligible. This criterion is subject to regular review.

### *Permanent Sequestration of Captured $CO_2$*

Operation of a permanent $CO_2$ storage facility is eligible if the facility complies with ISO 27914:2017 for geological storage of $CO_2$. These requirements are subject to periodic review.

## Transportation and storage

To achieve climate neutrality, a 90% reduction in transport emissions is needed by 2050 (compared to 1990). Road, rail, aviation, and waterborne transport will all need to contribute to the reduction[20]. Preliminary estimates from EU Member States show that GHG emissions from transport were 29% above 1990 levels in 2018[21].They now account for more than one quarter of the EU's total greenhouse gas emissions. Within the transport sector, road transport is the dominant emissions source, accounting for more than two-thirds (71.7%[22]) of transport-related greenhouse gas emissions. Passenger cars and vans are responsible for the bulk of these emissions, with the rest resulting from trucks and buses. Road transport is followed by shipping and aviation as the second and third largest sources of GHG emissions from transport.

For road vehicles there is a well-developed legislative framework in the EU that includes mandatory emissions testing. This system is most mature for cars and vans. It has recently evolved significantly for trucks, and buses are set to follow. Rail and inland waterways are also important emissions sources covered by the Taxonomy, ones which can provide modal shift benefits, relative to road and air. However, EU legislation provides less direct orientation regarding these modes of transport. The transport section of the climate mitigation Taxonomy deals primarily with climate mitigation activities relating to operations of vehicle/vessel fleets and the associated enabling infrastructure. The Taxonomy criteria for the manufacturing of vehicles and vessels are addressed in the manufacturing section of the Taxonomy.

There are several principal options[23] for climate mitigation in the transport sector, including:

- Increasing the number of low- and zero emission vehicles, improving vehicle efficiency and infrastructure
- Increasing substitution of fossil fuels with sustainable alternative and net-zero carbon fuels[24]
- Improving efficiency of the overall transport/mobility system.

The general Taxonomy approach for transport was inspired by the long-term strategic options for decarbonisation of the transport sector as per the Commission's long-term strategic vision 'A Clean Planet for All'[25]. Criteria developed for fleet efficiency and fuel substitution were designed to be discrete, and refer to relevant EU legislation. For fleet efficiency criteria, tank-to-wheel criteria were used since the basis for criteria is the Clean Vehicles Directive, the post-2020 $CO_2$ Regulation for cars and vans and the Heavy Duty $CO_2$ regulation. Life-cycle and well-to-wheel considerations for thresholds are pending a possible development of an agreement on a common Union methodology as per the above mentioned legislations.

In addition, it is noted in 'A Clean Planet for All' that land constraints imply that biofuels and bio methane should be deployed only in those transport modes or means where they are necessary. The scope of economic activities and the type of criteria proposed in this section may help to inform the design of technical criteria for the transport sector beyond the EU. However, the quantitative thresholds proposed are EU-focused by design given the EU Taxonomy regulation itself, but also because they are based on EU legal reference points.

At this stage, there are other activities in the transport sector that have not been addressed, but which need consideration as part of further work on the Taxonomy, e.g. by the Platform on Sustainable Finance.

These include:

- Maritime shipping (including reference to EU MRV regime)
- Aviation
- ICT for transport
- Energy efficiency improvements in equipment and infrastructure (e.g. in ports)
- Research, development & innovation related activities having the potential to substantially decarbonise the transport sector.

### *Passenger rail transport (interurban)*

- Zero direct emissions trains are eligible.
- Other trains are eligible if direct emissions (TTW) are below 50g $CO_2e$ emissions per passenger kilometre (g $CO_2e$/pkm) until 2025 (non-eligible thereafter).

Brief rationale: Zero direct emissions rail (e.g. electric, hydrogen) is eligible because:

- With the present energy mix, the overall emissions associated with zero direct emissions rail transport (i.e. electric or hydrogen) are among the lowest compared with other transport modes.
- The generation of the energy carriers used by zero direct emissions transport is assumed to become low or zero carbon in the near future.
- The threshold of 50g $CO_2e$/p/km until 2025 ensures that the carbon intensity remains similar to criteria for eligible road vehicles with low occupation factor (50g $CO_2$/vkm) and significantly lower than emissions for an average car in the current vehicle stock.

### *Freight rail transport*

- Zero direct emissions trains (e.g. hydrogen, electric) are eligible.
- Other trains are eligible if direct emissions per tonne-km (g $CO_2$ e/t/km) are 50% lower than average reference $CO_2$ emissions of HDVs as defined for the Heavy Duty $CO_2$ Regulation, to be reviewed in 2025.
- Rail that is dedicated to the transport of fossil fuels or fossil fuels blended with alternative fuels is not eligible even if meeting the criteria above.

Brief rationale: Zero direct emissions rail (e.g. electric, hydrogen) is eligible because:

- With the present energy mix, the overall emissions associated with zero direct emissions rail transport (i.e. electric or hydrogen) are among the lowest compared with other transport modes.
- The generation of the energy carriers used by zero direct emissions transport is assumed to become low or zero carbon in the near future.
- The threshold of 50% lower than average reference $CO_2$ emissions of HDVs ensures that the carbon intensity remains similar to criteria for eligible road freight vehicles, with a review in 2025 to assess technology developments in the freight transport sector. The Heavy Duty $CO_2$ Regulation uses a g $CO_2$/km metric. To convert this to a g$CO_2$/tonne-km metric, the average payload for the road freight vehicles should be applied. Once reference value data is available, it is expected that

the taxonomy will specify $CO_2e$/tkm threshold value generation of the energy carriers used by zero direct emissions transport is assumed to become low or zero carbon in the near future.

### *Public transport*

- Zero direct emissions land transport activities (e.g. light rail transit, metro, tram, trolleybus, bus and rail) are eligible.
- Other fleets are eligible if direct emissions are below 50 g $CO_2e$/p/km until 2025 (non-eligible thereafter)

Brief rationale: Zero direct emissions public transport (e.g. electric, hydrogen) is eligible because:

- With the present energy mix, the overall emissions associated with zero direct emissions public transport (i.e. electric or hydrogen) are among the lowest compared with other transport modes.
- The generation of the energy carriers used by zero direct emissions transport is assumed to become low or zero carbon in the near future.
- The threshold of 50 g $CO_2e$/p/km until 2025 ensures that the carbon intensity remains similar to criteria for eligible road vehicles with low occupation factor (50 g $CO_2$/v/km) and significantly lower than emissions for an average car.

### *Infrastructure for low carbon transport (land transport)*

The construction and operation of transport infrastructure is eligible in the following cases:

- Infrastructure that is required for zero direct emissions transport (e.g. electric charging points, electricity grid connection upgrades, hydrogen fuelling stations or electric highways).
- Infrastructure and equipment (including fleets) for active mobility (walking, cycling, e-bikes and e-scooters).
- Infrastructure that is predominantly used for low-carbon transport if the fleet that uses the infrastructure meets the thresholds for direct emissions as defined in the relevant activity - measured in $CO_2$ emissions per kilometre (g $CO_2$/km), $CO_2e$ emissions per tonne-kilometre (g $CO_2e$/t/km), or $CO_2e$ emissions per passenger-kilometre (g $CO_2$CO2e/p/km).
- Non-electrified rail infrastructure with an existing plan for electrification or use of alternatively powered trains.

For all cases:

- Only infrastructure that is fundamental to the operation of the transport service is eligible.
- Infrastructure that is dedicated to the transport of fossil fuels or blended fossil fuels is not eligible.

Brief Rationale: The construction and operation of infrastructure for low carbon land transport is considered eligible because this is considered a key enabling factor for improving the uptake of the transport activities that are considered eligible under the rest of the land transport section of the Taxonomy. Eligibility for infrastructure is linked to eligibility criteria for fleets using the infrastructure, with additional criteria relating to zero carbon transport (active mobility).

### *Passenger cars and commercial vehicles*

For passenger cars and light commercial vehicles:

- Zero tailpipe emission vehicles (incl. hydrogen, fuel cell, electric). These are automatically eligible.
- Vehicles with tailpipe emission intensity of max 50 g $CO_2$/km (WLTP) are eligible until 2025.
- From 2026 onwards only vehicles with emission intensity of 0g $CO_2$/km (WLTP) are eligible.

- For category L vehicles (e.g. motorcycles): Zero tailpipe emission vehicles (incl. hydrogen, fuel cell, electric).

Brief rationale: Zero direct emissions vehicles (e.g. electric, hydrogen) are eligible because the generation of the energy carriers used by zero tailpipe emissions vehicles is assumed to become low or zero carbon in the near future. Vehicles with tailpipe emission intensity of max 50 g $CO_2$/km (WLTP) are eligible until 2025 because the post-2020 $CO_2$ Regulation for cars and vans sets this threshold as an ambitious mid-term target that is significantly below the expected average emissions of new cars and vans. The 50 g $CO_2$/km threshold does not apply to L vehicles due to their lower weight and high electrification potential.

### *Freight transport services by road*

- Zero direct emission heavy-duty vehicles that emit less than 1g $CO_2$/kWh (or 1g $CO_2$/km for certain N2 vehicles) are automatically eligible;
- Low-emission heavy-duty vehicles with specific direct $CO_2$ emissions of less than 50% of the reference $CO_2$ emissions of all vehicles in the same sub-group are eligible.
- Dedicated vehicles solely using advanced biofuels or renewable liquid and gaseous transport fuels of non-biological origin as defined in Art. 2 (34) and Art. 2 (36) as well as low indirect land-use change-risk biofuels as defined in Art 2(37) in line with Directive (EU) 2018/2001), guaranteed either by technological design or ongoing monitoring and third-party verification. In addition, for an investment in new vehicles, only vehicles with efficiency corresponding to direct $CO_2$ emissions (g $CO_2$/ km) (biogenic $CO_2$) below the reference $CO_2$ emissions of all vehicles in the same sub-group are eligible. Eligibility should be reviewed latest by 2025.or when Directive (EU) 2018/2001) is reviewed.
- Fleets of vehicles dedicated to transport fossil fuels or fossil fuels blended with alternative fuels are not eligible. Brief rationale: Road freight transport with zero direct emissions vehicles (e.g. electric, hydrogen) is eligible because the generation of these energy carriers is assumed to become low or zero carbon in the near future. The definition is aligned with the heavy duty $CO_2$ regulation, which provides the most recent legislative point of reference. Road freight transport with low-emission heavy-duty vehicles defined in the same regulation and dedicated vehicles solely using a narrowly defined range of bio- or other renewable fuels are also eligible due to the relatively high challenges in electrifying this vehicle category. Substantial contribution to climate mitigation from fuel substitution is in line with the agreed Taxonomy regulation.

### *Interurban scheduled road transport*

- Zero tailpipe emission vehicles (incl. hydrogen, fuel cell, electric) are automatically eligible.
- Dedicated vehicles solely using advanced biofuels or renewable liquid and gaseous transport fuels of non-biological origin as defined in Art. 2 (34) and Art. 2 (36) in line with Directive (EU) 2018/2001), guaranteed either by technological design or ongoing monitoring and third-party verification. In addition, for an investment in new vehicles, only vehicles with efficiency corresponding to direct emissions below 95g $CO_2$ e /p/km (including biogenic $CO_2$) are eligible. Eligibility should be reviewed latest by 2025, or when Directive (EU) 2018/2001) is reviewed.
- Other vehicles are eligible if direct emissions are below 50 g $CO_2$e/p/km.

Brief rationale: Passenger transport with zero tailpipe emissions vehicles (e.g. electric, hydrogen) is eligible because the generation of these energy carriers is assumed to become low or zero carbon in the near future. Dedicated vehicles solely using a narrowly defined range of bio- or other renewable fuels are also eligible due to the relatively high challenges in electrifying the vehicle category typically used on interurban routes. Substantial contribution to climate mitigation from fuel substitution is in line with the agreed

Taxonomy regulation. The threshold of 50g $CO_2e$/p/km relates to the thresholds set for passenger cars (assuming occupancy of one) and represents a value that is significantly below average new car emissions.

### *Inland passenger water transport*

Zero direct emissions inland waterway vessels are eligible.

- Dedicated vessels solely using advanced biofuels or renewable liquid and gaseous transport fuels of non-biological origin as defined in Art. 2 (34) and Art. 2 (36) in line with Directive (EU) 2018/2001), guaranteed either by technological design or ongoing monitoring and third-party verification. In addition, for an investment in new vessels, only vessels with efficiency corresponding to direct emissions below 95g $CO_2$ e /p/km (including biogenic $CO_2$) are eligible. Eligibility should be reviewed latest by 2025, or when Directive (EU) 2018/2001) is reviewed.

Other Inland waterways vessels are eligible if direct emissions are below 50 g $CO_2e$ emissions per passenger kilometre (g $CO_2e$/p/km) (or 92.6 g per passenger nautical mile (g $CO_2e$/pnm)). Eligibility should be reviewed in 2025.

Brief Rationale: Zero direct emissions inland waterway transport (e.g. electric, hydrogen) is eligible because:

- With the present energy mix, the overall emissions associated with zero direct emissions rail transport (i.e. electric or hydrogen) are among the lowest compared with other transport modes.
- The generation of the energy carriers used by zero direct emissions transport is assumed to become low or zero carbon in the near future.

### *Inland freight water transport*

Zero direct emissions inland waterways vessels are eligible.

- Dedicated vessels solely using advanced biofuels or renewable liquid and gaseous transport fuels of non-biological origin as defined in Art. 2 (34) and Art. 2 (36) in line with Directive (EU) 2018/2001), guaranteed either by technological design or ongoing third-party monitoring and verification. In addition, for an investment in new vessels, only vessels with efficiency corresponding to direct $CO_2$ emissions (g $CO_2$/t/km) (including biogenic $CO_2$) below the average reference value defined for HDVs (Heavy Duty $CO_2$ Regulation) are eligible. Eligibility should be reviewed in 2025, or when Directive (EU) 2018/2001) is reviewed.
- Other inland waterway vessels are eligible if direct emissions per tkm $CO_2e$ emissions per tonne kilometre (g $CO_2e$/tkm) or per tonne nautical mile (g $CO_2e$/tnm) are 50% lower than the average reference value defined for HDVs (Heavy Duty $CO_2$ Regulation). Eligibility should be reviewed in 2025.
- Vessels that are dedicated to the transport of fossil fuels or any blended fossil fuels are not eligible even if meeting the criteria above.

Brief rationale: Zero direct emissions inland waterway transport (e.g. electric, hydrogen) is eligible because:

- With the present energy mix, the overall emissions associated with zero direct emissions waterways transport (i.e. electric or hydrogen) are among the lowest compared with other transport modes.
- The generation of the energy carriers used by zero direct emissions transport is assumed to become low or zero carbon in the near future. The threshold of 50% lower than average reference $CO_2$ emissions of HDVs ensures that the carbon intensity remains similar to criteria for eligible road freight vehicles, with a review in 2025 to assess technology developments in the freight transport

sector. The Heavy Duty $CO_2$ Regulation uses a g $CO_2$/km metric. To convert this to a g $CO_2$/tonne-km metric, the average payload for the road freight vehicles should be applied. Once reference value data is available, it is expected that the taxonomy will specify $CO_2e$/t/km threshold values. Substantial contribution to climate mitigation from fuel substitution is in line with the agreed taxonomy regulation.

### *Infrastructure for low carbon transport (water transport)*

The construction and operation of transport infrastructure is eligible in the following cases:

- Infrastructure that is required for zero direct emissions water transport (e.g. batteries or hydrogen fuelling facilities) is eligible.
- Infrastructure dedicated to supporting the renewable energy sector.
- Infrastructure that is predominantly used for low-carbon transport is eligible if the fleet that uses the infrastructure meets the thresholds for direct emissions as defined in the relevant activity - measured in $CO_2e$ emissions per passenger-kilometre (g $CO_2e$/p/km),per tonne-kilometre (g $CO_2e$/t/km), per passenger nautical mile (g $CO_2e$/pnm) or per tonne nautical mile (g $CO_2e$/t/nm)[26].

For all cases:

- Only infrastructure that is fundamental to the operation of the transport service is eligible.
- Infrastructure that is dedicated to the transport of fossil fuels or blended fossil fuels is not eligible.

Brief rationale: The construction and operation of infrastructure for low carbon water transport is considered eligible because this is considered a key enabling factor for improving the uptake of the transport activities that are considered eligible under the rest of the land transport section of the Taxonomy. Eligibility for infrastructure is linked to eligibility criteria for fleets using the infrastructure, with additional criteria relating to infrastructure supporting the renewable energy sector.

## Information and communications

This discussion focuses on NACE sector J – Information and Communication, which does not include electronics manufacturing. Based on the estimates published by the "European Framework Initiative for Energy & Environmental Efficiency in the ICT Sector"[27], the demand for telecommunications services is growing consistently. Internet Protocol (IP) traffic (data through telecom networks) has been estimated to be growing at a Compound Annual Growth Rate (CAGR) of 26 percent from 2017 to 2022[28].

The European Commission Joint Research Centre estimated total annual energy consumption of data centres in Western Europe as 56 TW/h (or 2% of the total electricity consumption) per year. In 2012, this was projected to increase to 104 TW/h (or 4%) per year by 2020. The large consumption of energy is due to the need for permanent storage of data (24 hour availability, back-up generators, etc.) and the need for cooling of the servers and other equipment to maintain optimal operating temperatures[29]. Given the complexity of data centres – which encompass hardware, software, cooling systems, monitoring and back-up energy systems, only to name a few components – and the trade-offs that are present in the industry between energy efficiency and reliability and security, a comprehensive approach was adopted. The "threshold" for significant contribution to mitigation is data centre compliance with the more advanced standard of energy efficiency available for this sector, the Best Practice Guidelines for the EU Code of Conduct on Data Centre Energy Efficiency (JRC) updated every year by the Commission to take account of technological advances[30].

In terms of sectors not yet covered under information and communications, the TEG recommends that the Commission undertake work on the following activities:

- Telecommunication networks
- Energy efficiency of software
- Context-specific digitalisation solutions for resource efficiency, or software applications that minimize resource consumption in other sectors of the economy. Examples include:
  - Transport: Electric-vehicle smart charging - manage Electric Vehicle charging stations smartly to leverage the extra storage capacity connected to the grid.
  - Agriculture: Precision agriculture digital solutions – allow, for example, for the right amount of water for irrigation, or fertiliser use.
  - Energy: Innovative grid equipment (e.g. short circuit breakers) to ensure security in grids with growing decentralised renewable production.

### *Data processing, hosting and related activities*

Threshold: The data centre implements the European Code of Conduct for Data Centre Energy Efficiency. This implies implementation of the practices described in the most recent "Best Practice Guidelines for the European Code of Conduct for Data Centre Energy Efficiency" (JRC) or in CEN/CENELEC documents CLC TR50600-99-1 and CLC TR50600-99-2.

### *Data-driven solutions for GHG emission reductions*

- The option to adopt a threshold for multi-purpose solutions (e.g. "50% of activity has to be applied to climate change") has been considered but rejected in light of the lack of control over the use of the data and analytics by the end user.
- The mix of NACE codes (telecommunication, software and data processing) is necessary to keep the category open to solutions that will emerge in the future.
- Exclusive use of data for climate change mitigation purposes is deemed sufficient to prove significant mitigation contribution and avoid application of thresholds.
- Example: Advanced weather forecasting models tailored to integrating more renewables in electricity generation. Digital technologies, such as machine-learning algorithms, when applied to weather and power plant output data, can increase the accuracy of renewable forecasts.
- Geographical scope: Global.

## Construction and real estate activities

Buildings are not a single economic activity under the NACE system. The TEG recognised that failure to address the carbon performance of buildings, which alone contribute 36% of $CO_{2e}$ emissions in the EU28[31], would risk causing harm to climate objectives. The TEG's buildings criteria are designed to be cross-cutting and apply across the economy, with the exception of explicitly excluded sectors (dedicated storage of fossil fuels). For presentation purposes, the TEG has aligned the building criteria with NACE codes for construction and real estate activities. However, the buildings criteria are not limited to these NACE codes and can be applied across other sectors and economic activities.

About three-quarters of European buildings are considered inefficient, and only 0.4-1.2% (depending on the country) of the building stock is renovated each year to improve its efficiency[32]. Renovation rates must be increased in order to put the building stock on a net-zero emissions pathway, while embodied and operational carbon emissions of new buildings must be significantly reduced in order to minimise their impact over their life cycle.

The Taxonomy distinguishes four 'economic activities' and defines consistent mitigation criteria that enable an eligibility assessment of investments in construction and real estate on the basis of their potential impact on building energy performance and thus carbon emissions.

Construction of new buildings: this activity covers real estate development and enables accounting of project capital expenditures of developers and construction clients as eligible 'low-carbon activities', as well as turnover of developers and contractors.

Building renovation: this activity covers comprehensive renovation and enables accounting of:

- Project capital expenditures for renovation as eligible 'transition activities':
  - When expenditures can be distinguished by type, at least 50% must be related to energy-efficiency measures in order to consider the renovation expenditures as eligible in their entirety[33].
  - When expenditures cannot be distinguished by type, 50% of the total renovation expenditures may be counted as the proxy representing energy-efficiency measures.
  - Turn-over of contractors.

Individual measures and professional services: this activity covers technical interventions aimed at increasing energy efficiency and professional services that are functional to energy improvements, and enables accounting of:

- Project capital expenditures of clients as eligible 'transition activities';
- Turn-over of installers and services providers.

Acquisition and ownership: this activity covers the purchase and management of buildings, and enables accounting of:

- Project capital expenditures of the buyer/owner as eligible 'transition activities' or 'low carbon activities' depending on building performance;
- Turnover of real estate brokers and facility managers.

The TEG faced several challenges to develop appropriate mitigation criteria for the construction and real estate sectors:

- The lack of consistent and comparable data across countries for benchmarking building stock performance and setting suitable thresholds for the top performing buildings within the respective national stock.
- The inherent difficulty of creating a level playing field across countries with different climates and degrees of market readiness.
- The desire to find a compromise between increasing ambition and building upon already existing 'green' financing instruments. The financing of buildings and building energy improvements is the most developed segment of the green finance market, and the ownership of buildings in portfolios is an extensively practiced economic activity. As the Taxonomy is introduced to the market, it is important to maintain the volume of existing investors and enable them to use the Taxonomy to evaluate their portfolios.
- The intention is to direct finance towards new buildings designed to higher standards than mandatory design and construction requirements, considering the varying levels of ambition and rigour regarding the implementation of nearly zero-energy buildings (NZEB) across EU Member States[34].

These principles led the TEG to develop the following criteria to identify environmentally sustainable activities in terms of substantial contribution to climate change mitigation:

Construction of new buildings: to be eligible, the design and construction of new buildings needs to ensure a net primary energy demand that is at least 20% lower than the level mandated by national regulations. This is assessed through the calculated energy performance of the building, i.e. performance forecasted on the basis of modelling building physics under typical climatic and occupancy conditions. This criterion is meant to be subject to reviews in the transitional decade 2020-2030 in order to take into account potential tightening of NZEB requirements by EU Member States, with the aim of setting the whole sector on a path to convergence with net-zero energy and carbon targets by 2030.

Building renovations: renovations designed to meet the local national or regional requirements for 'major renovation' as defined in the Energy Performance of Buildings Directive (EPBD)[35]; this will stimulate the market and encourage building owners undertaking a 'conventional' renovation to include energy-efficiency measures established by EU Member States in national and regional regulations implementing the EPBD. As an alternative, renovations are eligible if undertaken to ensure at least 30% savings in net primary energy demand in comparison to the baseline energy performance of the building before the renovation, assessed through the calculated energy performance of the building.

Individual measures and professional services: measures and services aimed at reducing energy and/or carbon emissions in buildings. This is assessed through technical requirements for each measure and service.

Acquisition and ownership: buildings built after 2021 are eligible if they meet the criteria for the 'Construction of new buildings', while buildings built before 2021 are eligible if their performance is comparable to the performance of the top 15% of the national stock, in terms of calculated Primary Energy Demand during the use phase. An additional requirement is applied only to large non-residential buildings (built both before and after 2021) to ensure efficient operations through energy management.

Outside the EU, the share of the market that could be eligible will also vary from country to country. Countries with ambitious building regulations that are accepted as Taxonomy-equivalent will more easily be able to make large shares of their market eligible. The principle of the top performing 15% of the national stock provides a methodology to demonstrate eligibility of the non-EU best in class building stock. For renovations, the 30% energy savings threshold (the alternative to the compliance with 'major renovation' requirements) will not only facilitate immediate functionality of the Taxonomy outside the EU, it will also make a significant part of renovation activities eligible, even in countries where national building regulations may not be ambitious enough. Moreover, the share of the market that could be eligible outside EU Member States will also depend on the local proliferation of Taxonomy-eligible sustainability certification schemes.

In terms of recommendations to the Commission for the next steps, methods and tools for embodied carbon assessment based on Life Cycle Assessment (LCA) are becoming more widespread. Notably, a large share of emissions embodied in buildings takes place during resource extraction and product manufacturing, before buildings are even occupied. This means that all new constructions begin their lifecycle with a significant amount of embodied carbon. The Sustainable Finance Platform could gather and analyse existing data in order to establish reliable thresholds for carbon emission embodied in new constructions, which would be integrated into the Taxonomy criteria for the activity 'Construction of new buildings' as additional threshold to be met.

### *Construction of new buildings*

The metric is Primary Energy Demand (PED), defining the energy performance of a building: the annual primary energy demand associated with regulated energy use during the operational phase of the building life-cycle (i.e. 'module B6' as defined in EN15978), calculated ex-ante according to the national methodologies for asset design assessment, or as defined in the set of standards ISO 52000, expressed as kWh/m$^2$ per year. The threshold is based on 'nearly zero-energy building' (NZEB) requirements, which are defined in national regulation implementing the EPBD and are mandatory for all new buildings across EU Member States from 2021.

To be eligible, the net primary energy demand of the new construction must be at least 20% lower than the primary energy demand resulting from the relevant NZEB requirements[36]. This reduction can be met through a direct decrease of the primary energy demand via a more efficient design or by offsetting with on-site and off-site renewable generation, or a combination of both strategies. Off-site energy generation must be limited to district heating and cooling systems and local renewable energy sources[37]. The methodology used for the measurement of floor area should be stated referring to the categories defined in the International Property Measurement Standards[38].

### *Building renovation*

The thresholds used to assess a renovation rely on either the respective metrics set in the applicable building energy performance regulation for 'major renovation' transposing the EPBD, or, in the case of relative improvement, on Primary Energy Demand (PED) defined as follows: the annual primary energy demand associated with regulated energy use during the operational phase of the building life-cycle (i.e. 'module B6' according to EN15978), calculated ex-ante according to the national methodologies for asset design assessment, or as defined in the set of standards ISO 52000, expressed as kWh/m2 per year.

A renovation is eligible when it meets either one of the following thresholds:

- Major renovation[39]: the renovation is compliant with the requirements set in the applicable building regulations for 'major renovation' transposing the Energy Performance of Buildings Directive (EPBD). The energy performance of the building or the renovated part upgraded must meet cost-optimal minimum energy performance requirements in accordance with the EPBD.
- Relative improvement: the renovation leads to reduction of Primary Energy Demand of at least 30% in comparison to the energy performance of the building before the renovation[40]. The initial energy performance and the estimated improvement shall be based on a specialised building survey and validated by an Energy Performance Certificate, an energy audit conducted by an accredited independent expert or any other transparent and proportionate method. The methodology used for the measurement of floor area should be stated referring to the categories defined in the International Property Measurement Standards[41].

### *Individual measures and professional services*

There are no defined metrics across the individual measures and professional services. The following individual measures are eligible if compliant with minimum requirements set for individual components and systems in the applicable national regulations transposing the Energy Performance Building Directive (EPBD), and must meet Ecodesign requirements pursuant to Directive 2009/125/EC:

- Addition of insulation to the existing envelope components, such as external walls, roofs (including green roofs), lofts, basements and ground floors (including measures to ensure air-tightness, measures to reduce the effects of thermal bridges and scaffolding) and products for the application of the insulation to the building envelope (mechanical fixings, adhesive, etc.).
- Replacement of existing windows with new energy efficient windows.
- Replacement of existing external doors with new energy efficient doors.
- Installation and replacement of heating, ventilation and air conditioning and domestic hot water systems, including equipment related to district heating service.
- Replacement of inefficient boiler or stove with highly efficient condensing boiler.

The following individual measures are eligible if specific requirements are met:

- Replacement of old pumps with efficient circulating pumps (as defined in Art. 2 of EU Regulation 622/2012).
- Installation of efficient LED lighting appliances and systems.
- Installation of low-flow kitchen and sanitary water fittings in the top two categories of the EU Water Label scheme.

The following individual measures are always eligible:

- Installation of zoned thermostats, smart thermostat systems and sensoring equipment, e.g. motion and day light control.
- Installation of Building Management Systems (BMS) and Energy Management Systems (EMS).
- Installation of charging stations for electric vehicles.
- Installation of smart meters for gas and electricity.
- Installation of façade and roofing elements with a solar shading or solar control function, including those that support the growing of vegetation.

The following individual measures are eligible if installed on-site as building services:

- Installation of solar photovoltaic systems (and the ancillary technical equipment).
- Installation of solar hot water panels (and the ancillary technical equipment).
- Installation and upgrade of heat pumps contributing to the targets for renewable energy in heating and cooling in accordance with Directive 2018/2001/EU (and the ancillary technical equipment).
- Installation of wind turbines (and the ancillary technical equipment).
- Installation of solar transpired collectors (and the ancillary technical equipment).
- Installation of thermal or electric energy storage units (and the ancillary technical equipment).
- Installation of High Efficiency Micro CHP (combined heat and power) plant
- Installation of heat exchanger/recovery systems.

The following professional services are eligible:

- Technical consultations (energy consultants, energy simulation, project management, production of EPC, dedicated training, etc.) linked to the individual measures mentioned above.
- Accredited energy audits and building performance assessments.
- Energy Management Services.
- Energy Performance Contracts.
- Energy Services provided by Energy Service Companies (ESCOs).

### *Acquisition and ownership*

The metric is Primary Energy Demand (PED): the annual primary energy demand associated with regulated energy use during the operational phase of the building life-cycle (i.e. 'module B6' according to EN15978), calculated ex-ante according to the national methodologies for asset design assessment, or as defined in the set of standards ISO 52000, expressed as kWh/m$^2$ per year.

**Case A – Acquisition of buildings built before 31 December 2020**

The calculated performance of the building must be within the top 15% of the local existing stock in terms of operational Primary Energy Demand, expressed as kWh/m$^2$/year. Alignment with this criterion can be demonstrated by providing adequate evidence comparing the performance of the relevant asset to the performance of the local stock built before 31 December 2020. Such evidence should be based on a representative sample of the building stock in the respective area where the building is located, distinguishing at the very least between residential and non-residential buildings. The area can be defined as a city, a region or a country. Certification schemes such as EPCs may be used as evidence of eligibility when adequate data is available to demonstrate that a specific level (e.g. EPC A) clearly falls within the top 15% of the respective local stock. Large non-residential buildings must meet an additional requirement: efficient building operations must be ensured through dedicated energy management[42].

**Case B – Acquisition of buildings built after 31 December 2020**

The building must meet the criteria established for the 'Construction of new buildings' that are relevant at the time of the acquisition. Large non-residential buildings must meet an additional requirement: efficient building operations must be ensured through dedicated energy management.

## References

EUOFFICIALJOURNAL (2020), *https://eur-lex.europa.eu/legal-content/EN/TXT/PDF/?uri=CELEX:32020R0852&from=EN*. [2]

European Commission (2020), *https://ec.europa.eu/eurostat/ramon/nomenclatures/index.cfm?TargetUrl=LST_NOM_DTL&StrNom=CL_CEPAREM&StrLanguageCode=EN&IntPcKey=&StrLayoutCode=HIERARCHIC#:~:text=RAMON%20%2D%20Reference%20And%20Management%20Of%20Nomenclatures&text=Classification%20of%20Re*. [5]

European Commission (2020), *https://ec.europa.eu/eurostat/statistics-explained/index.php/Glossary:Classification_of_environmental_protection_activities_(CEPA)*. [4]

EuropeanCommission (2018), *EC Regulation on the establishment of a framework to facilitate sustainable investment*, https://eur-lex.europa.eu/legal-content/EN/TXT/PDF/?uri=CELEX:52018PC0353&from=EN. [1]

Eurostat (2016), *https://ec.europa.eu/eurostat/statistics-explained/index.php/Climate_change_-_driving_forces#Total_emissions.2C_main_breakdowns_by_source_and_general_drivers*. [7]

OECD (2019), *Accelerating Climate Action: Refocusing Policies through a Well-being Lens*, OECD Publishing, Paris, https://dx.doi.org/10.1787/2f4c8c9a-en. [6]

Stiglitz, J., J. Fitoussi and M. Durand (2018), *Beyond GDP: Measuring What Counts for Economic and Social Performance*, OECD Publishing, Paris, https://dx.doi.org/10.1787/9789264307292-en. [3]

## Notes

[1] Reference to Article 1 of the Regulation.

[2] Nomenclature des Activités Economiques dans la Communauté Européenne (NACE) is a European industry standard classification system which feeds into several EC economic and statistical systems, e.g. at Eurostat level.

[3] For example, by Eurostat

[4] Pages 85 to 95 of the TEG report contain an attempt of mapping of the stock of bonds and shares held by ECB against the taxonomy, also see table below. This study shows the significant proportion of financial products currently recorded under NACE codes "finance" and "services" in ECB databases. The taxonomy was developed for "real economy" sectors only and is therefore silent on those stocks, when the taxonomy is used this way.

[5] Funds subject to the EC's regulatory framework for "Undertakings for the Collective Investment in Transferable Securities".

[6] An Exchange Traded Fund (ETF) is a basket of securities that tracks an underlying index.

[7] Funds investing in any asset class excluding stocks, bonds, and cash.

[8] Based on the EU ETS benchmark for grey cement clinker. The threshold for cement clinker needs to be revised every time that there is an update in the EU ETS benchmark value for grey cement clinker.

[9] A detailed explanation of the threshold calculation is provided p 206 of the Technical Annex to the TEG final report on the EU taxonomy.

[10] The power density approach has been proposed to ease the administrative burden for conducting PCFs.

[11] https://www.hydropower.org/gres

[12] 250 as described in the 'Guidelines for the Quantitative Analysis of Net GHG Emissions from Reservoirs', issued in 2 volumes (Measurement Programmes & Data Analysis, and Modelling: Guidelines for Quantitaitve Analysis of Net GHG Emissions from Reservoirs)

[13] 252 Direct emissions of carbon dioxide (and to a lesser extent methane) result from the release of naturally occurring non-condensable gases (NCGs) from the geothermal fluid during the energy extraction process.

[14] A system is defined as the transmission or distribution network control area of the network or system operator(s) where the activity takes place. The European system shall be defined as the interconnected electricity system covering the interconnected control areas of EU Member States, Norway, Switzerland and the United Kingdom.

[15] Directive 2009/125/EC of the European Parliament and of the Council of 21 October 2009 establishing a framework for the setting of ecodesign requirements for energy-related products.

[16] See https://en.wikipedia.org/wiki/Allam_power_cycle

[17] Value of 0.5 according to the European benchmarking. Public Report IB2017 in https://www.waterbenchmark.org/documents/Public-documents

[18] The Infrastructure Leakage Index (ILI) is calculated as current annual real losses (CARL) / unavoidable annual real losses (UARL). See Canfora P., Antonopoulos I. S., Dri M., Gaudillat P., Schönberger H. (2019), "Best Environmental Management Practice for the Public Administration Sector". JRC Science for Policy Report EUR 29705 EN.

[19] For definition of fertilising products refer to ANNEX I of Proposed Regulation COM (2016) 157 laying down rules on the making available on the market of EU fertilising products, amending Regulations (EC) No 1069/2009 and (EC) No 1107/2009 and repealing Regulation (EC) No 2003/2003

[20] The European Green Deal, COM(2019) 640 final (include link)

[21] https://www.eea.europa.eu/themes/transport/term/increasing-oil-consumption-and-ghg

[22] Greenhouse gas emissions from transport:

https://ec.europa.eu/transport/facts-fundings/statistics/pocketbook-2019_en

[23] '"A Clean Planet for All". A European long-term strategic vision for a prosperous, modern, competitive and climate neutral economy'.https://ec.europa.eu/clima/sites/clima/files/docs/pages/com_2018_733_analysis_in_support_en_0.pdf.

[24] The European Green Deal, COM(2019) 640 final

[25] "A Clean Planet for All". A European long-term strategic vision for a prosperous, modern, competitive and climate neutral economy'.
https://ec.europa.eu/clima/sites/clima/files/docs/pages/com_2018_733_analysis_in_support_en_0.pdf.

[26]At this stage, only criteria for inland waterway transport passenger and freight fleets are defined. The criteria for infrastructure could not be applied to non-zero direct emissions maritime shipping fleets until criteria for that type of activity is defined.

[27] https://ictfootprint.eu/en/about/ict-carbon-footprint/ict-carbon-footprint

[28] Cisco Annual Internet Report (2018-2023) – Updated on 28 February 2020 - https://www.cisco.com/c/en/us/solutions/collateral/executive-perspectives/annual-internet-report/white-paper-c11-741490.html

[29] EC JRC, Best Environmental Management Practice in the Telecommunications and ICT Services Sector, 2016 available at http://susproc.jrc.ec.europa.eu/activities/emas/documents/TelecomICT_BEMP_BackgroundReport.pdf

[30] The 2019 version is available at this link: https://e3p.jrc.ec.europa.eu/publications/2019-best-practice-guidelines-eu-code-conduct-data-centre-energy-efficiency

[31] https://ec.europa.eu/energy/en/topics/energy-efficiency/energy-performance-of-buildings

[32] https://ec.europa.eu/energy/en/eu-buildings-database

[33] Certain types of financial instruments such as loans for acquisition and renovation of buildings may need to consider acquisition costs integrally with the eligible renovation costs if these costs cannot be practically separated in those types of financial instruments.

[34] According to Article 9 of the EPBD, by 31 December 2020 all new buildings must be NZEB.

[35] 412 According to Article 7 of the Energy Performance in Buildings Directive, buildings undergoing major renovation must meet the cost-optimal minimum energy performance requirements.

[36] The PED is either directly expressed by NZEB requirements or is derived by applying those requirements and calculating the resulting PED. When NZEB requirements specify a PED, the percentage improvement should be applied to this figure.

[37] As defined in national methodologies developed by EU Member States to implement the EPBD.

[38] International Property Measurement Standards (IPMS): https://ipmsc.org/

[39] Major renovation' means the renovation of a building where:

(a) the total cost of the renovation relating to the building envelope or the technical building systems is higher than 25 % of the value of the building, excluding the value of the land upon which the building is situated; or

(b) more than 25 % of the surface of the building envelope undergoes renovation. Member States may choose to apply option (a) or (b).

[40] The 30% improvement must result from an actual reduction in primary energy demand (i.e. reductions in net primary energy demand through renewable energy sources do not count), and can be achieved through a succession of measures within a maximum of 3 years.

[41] International Property Measurement Standards (IPMS): https://ipmsc.org/

[42] Regulation (EC) No 1907/2006 of the European Parliament and of the Council of 18 December 2006 concerning the Registration, Evaluation, Authorization and Restriction of Chemicals (REACH)

# 8 Sustainable finance definitions in Japan

This chapter provides background on the guidelines for green bonds, green loans and sustainability linked loans. These definitions are principle-based and contain guidance on metrics.

## 8.1. History and present status of sustainable finance definitions in Japan

### *8.1.1. Introduction*

In the case of Japan, no legislative definition falls into the strict category of a "taxonomy". Japan has not issued a sovereign green bond. The sustainable finance guidelines issued so far by the Japanese authorities are principle-based, they contain metrics guidance but no thresholds.

Japan, the world's third largest economy, is home to some of the most powerful financial institutions in the world. It also boasts one of the main global financial centres, Tokyo. As host country, Japan was instrumental in concluding international negotiations in 1997 on the Kyoto Protocol under the UN Framework Convention on Climate Change (UNFCCC). The Bank of Japan is a member of the Central Banks Network for Greening the Financial System (NGFS). Emerging sustainable finance practices in Japan include increasing consideration of environmental, social, and governance (ESG) criteria in financial decision-making and the development of green bond and sustainable investment markets (Schumacher, Chenet and Volz, 2020[1]) . Between 2016 and 2018, Japanese investment in sustainable assets increased 307 percent, outpacing other countries and Europe. One publicly owned institution that has played a crucial role in promoting ESG in Japan is the Government Pension Investment Fund (GPIF), the world's largest pension fund, which was created in 2006, managing over JPY 159 trillion (Japanese yen) as of 31 March 2019. In 2017, the GPIF adopted an ESG investment strategy and selected ESG indices. In December 2018, the GPIF expressed its support for the Task Force for Climate-related Financial Disclosures (TCFD) recommendations.

In addition, many Japanese financial actors are seeing benefits in increased climate risk assessment and transparency. At the end of 2018, The Ministry of Economy, Trade and Industry (METI) declared its support for the TCFD Recommendations and released its TCFD Guidance to show companies the first steps that they should take in starting information disclosures in accordance with the TCFD Recommendations (METI, 2018[2]). As of December 2019, the number of organisations supporting the recommendations of the Task Force on Climate-Related Financial Disclosures (TCFD) stood at 930 worldwide (FSB, 2019[3]). As of 6 March 2020, 240 organisations from Japan had joined the Japan TCFD Consortium (TCFD, 2020[4]), making it the world's largest such consortium.

### *8.1.2. The sustainable investment market*

Despite significant market growth rates in recent years, the size of Japan's sustainable finance markets is still relatively low in comparison to other countries. As of 19 April 2020, 84 Japanese organisations had signed up to the Principles for Responsible Investment (PRI). This compares to 2954 PRI signatories in the rest of the world. Japan's sustainable investment under management was JPY 263 trillion (USD 2.4 billion) at the beginning of 2018, compared with USD 14.1 trillion in Europe and USD 12.0 trillion in the U.S. (GSIA, 2018[5]).

### *8.1.3. The green bond market*

Japan's green bond market is the ninth largest globally and the second largest in the Asia-Pacific region after China with its cumulative issuance amounting to ¥1,875bn (US$17bn) as of end-2019. Green bond issuance for 2019 recorded a 70% increase compared to 2018, totalling ¥786.7bin. Financial corporates dominate the market, accounting for 50% of issuance (¥938.8bn). The Japanese market has a high proportion of external reviews with about 90% of its issuance with 60% of deals by volume benefiting from a Second Party Opinion (SPO) and 21% with at least a green bond rating (CBI, 2019[6]).

As for use of proceeds, buildings dominate cumulative proceed allocations at 38%. Significant contributions in this sector came from the Development Bank of Japan (cumulative ¥188.3bn), while Japan Housing

Finance Agency (¥70bn) represented the largest green buildings issuer in 2019. Energy (29%) and transport (25%) follow, with financial corporate Mitsubishi UFG Financial Group (¥216.3bn) and government-backed entity JRTT (¥197bn) representing the top issuers in the respective sectors. The Tokyo Metropolitan Government is the first Japanese issuer to allocate proceeds to adaptation and resilience, with cumulative ¥13.5bn earmarked towards flood prevention mechanisms. Japanese issuers prefer shorter tenors with 57% of bonds having a tenor of up to five years while 27% falling in the 'five-to-ten years' category. Ten percent of volumes have a tenor of more than 20 years. Issuance from the Development Bank of Japan and around 50% of non-financial corporates volumes have tenors of up to five years. The same tenor bucket is also the most popular amongst financial corporates, with almost 60% (¥178.7bn) of proceeds from Mitsubishi UFG maturing within five years. In terms of international comparability, most green bonds issued to date (above 80%) have received a second opinion and are consistent with the Climate Bonds Initiative Taxonomy. Currently external reviewer Sustainalytics (now owned by Morningstar) has a major share of the Japanese Green bond market, with other players such as DNV GNL, Vigeo Eiris (now owned by Moody's) or ISS OEkom (now owned by S&P) present as well.

Japan has various certification schemes for energy efficiency and performance in buildings that allow for the identification of low carbon buildings. The Japan House Finance Agency entered the green bond market in early 2019, through the securitisation of residential mortgages under the "Flat 35S" efficiency scheme. This is the same kind of structure as that used in the U.S. by the Federal National Mortgage Association ("Fannie Mae") to issue green bonds. Fannie Mae Green Bonds are green mortgage-backed securities (MBS) created through the aggregation and securitisation of green mortgages (home loans). Eligibility requirements for loans include reduction of the property's annual energy usage by at least 15%, and combined energy and or water savings of at least 30% (Fannie Mae, 2019[7]).

### *8.1.4. Sustainable finance definitions*

In 2017, the Ministry of the Environment of Japan (MOEJ) launched Japan's green bond guidelines. The aim was to promote the further spread of domestic green bonds while ensuring the reliability of the environmental effects of green bonds and reducing the costs and administrative burdens for issuers, as well as consistency with the International Capital Markets Association (ICMA) Green Bond Principles. The 2017 guidelines were principle-based and do not contain strict eligibility criteria or thresholds. The green bond guidelines were revised in 2020 to account for the revision of the ICMA Green Bond Principles, and to include more products. They are presented in more detail below (MOEJ, 2020[8]). For its part, the Ministry of Economy, Trade and Industry of Japan (METI) also issued a good practice guide for climate adaptation by the Japanese private sector, which consists of 20 one-sheet summaries of model corporate adaptation policies.

## 8.2. Objectives and scope of the 2020 green bond, green loan and sustainability linked loan guidelines

In its 2020 revision of te green bond guidelines – renamed the 2020 Green Bond, and Green Loan and Sustainability Linked Loan guidelines (henceforth JGBG&GLSLL) -- the MOEJ was attentive to the provision of funds for green projects not only by bonds but also by loans. It also introduced sustainability-linked loans, which are loans where financing conditions, such as the level of interest rate, are reviewed in line with the progress of the borrower on pre-determined Sustainability Performance Targets (SPTs). Experimentation with loans involving variable financing conditions was undertaken in Japan as far back as in 2004, when the Development Bank of Japan provided the first environmentally rated loan, ahead of other countries. The JGB&GLSLL aim at encouraging corporate behaviour, via finance, to become environmentally friendly, and developing green finance markets via voluntary adoption. In particular, they recognize that "green bonds are becoming an effective tool to raise funds for green projects, such as those contributing to the reduction of greenhouse gas (GHG) emissions and the prevention of natural capital deterioration. This trend became noticeable after the establishment of the Green Bond Principles (GBP) with the support of the International Capital Market Association (ICMA) in January 2014. Green Bond issuances and investments started to be seen in Japan as well. The spread of Green Bonds in Japan, however, is slow in comparison with other countries. (MOEJ, 2020, p. 15[8])". The general aim of the guidelines can be summarized as securing the credibility of green characteristics of the use of proceeds (i.e. seeking to avoid green washing), while alleviating the costs and administrative burdens for issuers. They also seek to spur knowledge accumulation in the market, by encouraging investors to disclose, and having the market evaluate the information disclosed by the issuer.

The 2020 JGBG&GLSLL are consistent with the ICMA Green Bond Principles and consistent with the Green Loan Principles and Sustainability Linked Loan Principles formulated in 2018 and 2019 respectively by the Loan Market Association (LMA). The guidelines also refer to other international classifications, including the EU Taxonomy, as potential additional, complementary tools: "It should be noted that international efforts are being made to classify environmentally sustainable economic activities in order to specify the eligible recipients of investments and loans in sustainable finance. This classification could function as an additional reference document regarding issuers who, for instance, wish to issue bonds in a bond market in the region that takes part in such efforts and will help investors identify eligible green projects" (MOEJ, 2020, p. 14[8]). The next sections set out the guidelines for each product (green bonds, green loans, and sustainability linked loans.

### 8.2.1. Objectives and scope of the 2020 green bond guidelines (JGBG)

The JGBG define green bonds as "bonds issued by companies, local governments, or other organizations to raise funds for domestic and overseas green projects" (MOEJ, 2020, p. 16[8]). The projects financed should not have "serious negative social impacts" (MOEJ, 2020, p. 17[8]). "Sustainability bonds are any type of bond instrument where the proceeds will be exclusively applied to finance or refinancing a combination of green and social projects, and which align with the four core components of the Green Bond Principles and/or Social Bond Principles (SBP)". The guidelines for green bonds also apply to sustainability bonds. The guidelines state that green bonds are expected to incorporate and reflect four components:

- Use of proceeds
- Process for project evaluation and selection
- Management of proceeds
- Reporting and (5) External review

*Use of proceeds*

- The green bonds proceeds should be allocated to green projects that have clear environmental benefits, with a recommendation to quantify them if possible, and some indications to that effect, as detailed below.
- Use of proceeds may include research and development expenses, human resources education expenses and monitoring expenses in connection with such projects.

The guidelines provide an indicative, non-exhaustive sector list summarised below:

- Renewable energy (including generation, transmission, appliances, and products)
- Energy efficiency (such as new and refurbished energy efficient buildings, energy storage, district heating, smart grids, appliances and products)

- Pollution prevention and control (including waste water treatment, GHG control, soil remediation, "3R-based" (reduce, reuse, recycle) waste management and waste-to-energy, and associated environmental monitoring analysis)
- Sustainable management of living natural resources and land use (including environmentally sustainable agriculture, fishery, aquaculture, and forestry, integrated pest management, weed management, and drip-irrigation)
- Projects for terrestrial and aquatic biodiversity conservation (including the protection of coastal, marine, and watershed environments)
- Projects for clean transportation (such as energy efficient next-generation vehicles, public transportation, railways, bicycles, non-motorized, multi-modal transportation, infrastructure for clean energy vehicles and the reduction of harmful emissions)
- Projects for sustainable water management (including sustainable infrastructure for clean and/or drinking water, sustainable urban drainage systems, and river draining and other forms of flood mitigation)
- Projects for climate change adaptation (including information support systems, such as climate observation and early warning systems)
- Projects concerning eco-efficient products, production technologies, and processes (including the development and introduction of environmentally friendlier, eco labelled, or certified products, and packaging using recyclable or renewable resources or other materials which reduce environmental loading)
- Projects to newly build or renovate green buildings that not only are energy efficient but also address a wide range of issues for consideration such as water consumption or waste management. Compliance with domestic standards or with an environmental certification that demonstrates a high level of efficiency in the environmental certification system, such as LEED[1] and CASBEE[2], is sought.

The guidelines recognise that some green projects may have incidental negative impacts on the environment, in addition to their intended environmental benefits. In such cases, the guidelines prescribe that those negative environmental impacts are evaluated by the issuers as limited compared to their environmental benefits, and that the issuers should include information regarding these negative impacts (e.g., how they are assessed, what the issuers will do to curb them) to investors so that the investors and market participants can appropriately evaluate these impacts. The guidelines propose examples of such negative impacts for each broad category of eligible projects. Examples provided for a solar power generation project include (MOEJ, 2020, p. 75[8]) :

- Ecological disruption or adverse effects on ecosystems caused by massive land development
- Outflow of muddy water
- Spilling of soil such as topsoil
- Light pollution and adverse effect on scenery
- Noise and vibration from the relevant facilities.

### *8.2.2. Process for project evaluation and selection*

Issuers should inform investors of the environmental sustainability objectives they intend to achieve with the green bonds and the criteria for selecting the projects accordingly. Examples of environmental objectives are climate change mitigation, adaptation, and the conservation of biodiversity. For climate change mitigation, the criterion can be GHG emissions reductions.

*Management of proceeds*

The issuer should conduct periodic checks (at least yearly) to ensure that the amount allocated to green projects is equal to or greater than the amount raised by the issuance of green bonds.

*Reporting*

Issuers should disclose how the funds are used at least once a year until all the proceeds are used and whenever there has been a major change in the situation. More specifically, disclosure methods may include disclosing environmental benefits per project, such as the amount of carbon dioxide reduced per year.

*External review*

It is recommended that issuers provide an external review. External reviewers should follow professional ethical standards, including integrity, fairness, ability and due care.

### 8.2.3. Objectives and scope of the 2020 green loan guidelines (GL)

The Green Loan Principles (hereinafter referred to as "GLP") were published in March 2018 by the Loan Market Association (LMA) and the Asia Pacific Loan Market Association (APLMA)[3]. The Japan Green Loan Guidelines state that "proceeds should be allowed exclusively to green projects, tracked and managed in a reliable manner, and transparency should be ensured by reporting after the issuance of the bonds" (MOEJ, 2020, p. 45[8]). The guidelines signal that this framework could become an effective tool to attract private funding to businesses that contribute to the reduction of GHG emissions and prevention of natural capital deterioration in Japan. The guidelines state that a green loan is expected to incorporate and reflect four components:

- Use of proceeds
- Process for project evaluation and selection
- Management of proceeds
- Reporting

The criteria are very similar to those for green bonds above.

### 8.2.4. Objectives and scope of the 2020 sustainability linked loans guidelines (SLL)

The guidelines also refer to the sustainability linked loan principles (referred to below as "SLLP") formulated in March 2019 by the Loan Markets Association (LMA), the Loan Syndications and Trading Association (LSTA) and the Asia Pacific Loan Markets Association (APLMA), in order to promote sustainable economic activities. A sustainability-linked loan (SLL) is a loan that encourages borrowers to achieve ambitious sustainability performance targets (SPTs). Specifically, it is a loan that: (1) organises the relationships between sustainability objectives and SPTs set out in the borrowers' comprehensive social responsibility strategies; (2) measures the degree of improvement in sustainability by setting appropriate SPTs; and (3) ensures transparency through post-loan reporting on SPTs. Unlike green loans, SLLs are often used for general business purposes, not limited to specific projects. The SLLP provide a framework that ties improvement of sustainability performance of borrower companies, to loan terms (such as interest). The guidelines mention that SLLs can be a tool for promoting governance, strategies and risk management systems for sustainability within businesses and throughout their supply chains, as well as for meeting voluntary ESG information disclosure requirements recommended by the Task Force on Climate-related Financial Disclosures (TCFD) and others. SLLs are expected to contain four components:

- Reconciling the relationship between the borrower's sustainability goals and sustainable performance target (SPTs)
- Setting of appropriate SPTs and measurement of sustainability
- Reporting
- External review

*Borrowers' sustainability goals*

The Borrower of an SLL should inform the lender that the sustainability objectives set out in its comprehensive social responsibility strategies are consistent with the SPTs.

*SPT measurement*

Borrowers are invited to select one or more Sustainability Coordinator(s) or Sustainability Structuring Agent(s) to help them negotiate SPTs setting. The SPTs includes key performance metrics (KPIs), external ratings, and comparable metrics to measure the borrowers' improvement in sustainability. The SPTs should be ambitious and refer to a business line of activity, which is material to the borrower. They should also be quantitative and based on recent data (less than one year). Typically, lending conditions are tied to performance achievement, with the interest rate lowered if the SPTs are met, or raised if the targets are not met.

*Reporting*

Reporting should be at least yearly. Where feasible, ESG ratings by external agencies related to the achievement of SPTs can be provided.

*External review*

The need for External Review is determined by agreement between Borrowers and lenders.

## 8.3. Metrics and thresholds

### *8.3.1. Metrics for measuring environmental effects*

The guidelines provide numerous examples of indicative metrics and methodologies for measuring and disclosing the environmental effects of green projects. But they don't provide eligibility thresholds within categories. Examples of indicative metrics provided are shown below:

*Renewable energy*

- Reduction in $CO_2$ emissions ($tCO_2$)
- Electricity generated by renewable energy (GWh)
- Renewable energy utilization rate in manufacturing process (percentage)

*Energy conservation*

- Reduction in $CO_2$ emissions ($tCO_2$)
- Reduction in energy consumption (k/L, t, m3, MWh)

## 8.4. Outlook and next steps

In March 2020, the METI's Study Group on Environmental Innovation Finance published a concept paper (METI, 2020[9]) on Climate Transition Finance Principles. Those principles call for further climate action aligned with the Paris Agreement. The tendency in sustainable finance in Japan has been to increasingly emphasize transparency and impact and an increase in the issue of transition bonds could ensue as a logical consequence, particularly in the context of the financing needs of the recovery from Covid-19.

## References

CBI (2019), *https://www.climatebonds.net/files/reports/cbi_japan_gfsotm2019.pdf.* [6]

Fannie Mae (2019), *https://multifamily.fanniemae.com/sites/g/files/koqyhd161/files/2019-10/green-mbs-at-glance.pdf.* [7]

FSB (2019), *https://www.fsb-tcfd.org/tcfd-supporters/.* [3]

GSIA (2019), *http://www.gsi-alliance.org/wp-content/uploads/2019/03/GSIR_Review2018.3.28.pdf.* [10]

GSIA (2018), *http://www.gsi-alliance.org/wp-content/uploads/2019/03/GSIR_Review2018.3.28.pdf.* [5]

IBEC (2020), *http://www.ibec.or.jp/CASBEE/english/.* [11]

METI (2020), *https://www.meti.go.jp/press/2019/03/20200331002/20200331002-2.pdf.* [9]

METI (2018), *https://www.meti.go.jp/english/press/2018/1225_006.html.* [2]

MOEJ (2020), *https://www.env.go.jp/policy/guidelines_set_version_with cover.pdf.* [8]

Schumacher, K., H. Chenet and U. Volz (2020), "Sustainable finance in Japan", *Journal of Sustainable Finance & Investment*, Vol. 10/2, pp. 213-246, http://dx.doi.org/10.1080/20430795.2020.1735219. [1]

TCFD (2020), *https://tcfd-consortium.jp/en/member_list.* [4]

## Notes

[1] LEED stands for Leadership in Energy and Environmental Design. It is a certification programme for Green Buildings developed by the U.S. Green Building Council that started in the U.S. It assesses the energy efficiency and other comprehensive environmental load of buildings. There are four certification levels—standard, silver, gold, and platinum.

[2] CASBEE stands for the Comprehensive Assessment System for Built Environment Efficiency, which is the green building management system in Japan. This system was developed by a research committee established in 2001 through the collaboration of academia, industry and national and local governments, which established the Japan Sustainable Building Consortium (JSBC) under the auspice of the Ministry of Land, Infrastructure, Transport and Tourism (MLIT). Various CASBEE schemes are now deployed all over Japan and supported by national and local governments. Under the system, buildings are evaluated and rated according to their environmental performance based on their building quality comprehensively, evaluating not only the use of energy efficient and environmentally-friendly materials, but also interior comfort and harmony with the surroundings. The evaluation results are rated on a scale of one to five levels ranging from S rank (excellent) to C rank (inferior) (IBEC, 2020[11]).

[3] The LMA is the trade body for the Europe, Middle East and African syndicated loan market and was founded in December 1996 by banks operating in that market. It develops standards of documentation and codes of market practice. The APLMA and LSTA are equivalent organisations in Asia and the USA respectively.

# 9 Sustainable finance definitions and taxonomies in China

China issued several legislative frameworks in relation to sustainable finance. The green bond catalogue issued by the People's Bank of China in 2015 is often referred to as China's taxonomy. China also issued a "Guiding catalogue for the green industry", updated in 2019. For lending, the China Banking Regulatory Commission issued green credit guidelines, performance indicators and reporting forms.

## 9.1. History and present status of sustainable finance definitions and taxonomies in China

### 9.1.1. Introduction

In the case of China, no legislative definition falls into the strict category of a "taxonomy" comparable to that of the EU. China has not issued a sovereign green bond. The green credit regulations in China provide some metrics but no thresholds, and the green bond regulations do not contain metrics or thresholds. The legislative frameworks are reviewed below. It is worth noting that the green bond catalogue issued in 2015 by the People's Bank of China (PBOC) is usually referred to as "a taxonomy".

China is a pioneer on green and sustainable finance. As the largest economy in the world, its efforts to develop and apply sustainable finance definitions, build sustainable finance markets, and shift investment from environmentally unsustainable to sustainable activities will be essential to meeting global environmental objectives.

China is the largest coal consumer and emitter of greenhouse gases in the world. High levels of local air pollution have become a significant concern. In 2006, the Chinese government decided to promote environmental insurance strongly. In 2007, the 17th national congress of the Communist Party of China proposed in 2007 the construction of an "eco-civilization". In 2008, the government started national trial applications of pollution insurance in several cities and provinces (Feng et al., 2013[1]). Since then, environmental issues have received even more attention.

China is actively engaged in international cooperation regarding climate change and climate finance. China approved the Paris Agreement and set up its Nationally Determined Contribution on June 30, 2015 (UNFCCC, 2015[2]), in which it committed that its carbon dioxide emissions would peak around 2030 and carbon dioxide emissions per unit of GDP in 2030 would be 60% to 65% lower than in 2005. At the One Planet Summit in December 2017, China joined the Central Banks Network for Greening the Financial System (NGFS). China also started to implement its 2013 Belt and Road Initiative (BRI) strategy (Wikipedia, 2020[3]). The BRI focuses mainly on mobilising capital for infrastructure investments and improvement of the connectivity of nations, most of which are still relatively low income (Vivid Economics, 2019, p. 4[4]). The BRI involves 126 countries representing about 28% of global carbon emissions in 2015. "China is proposing a holistic implementation of the BRI, covering a number of broad aspects that will be important for achieving the 2030 sustainable development goals" " (OECD, 2018, p. 13[5]). Aspects of this much broader approach include ecology and the environment including green and low carbon development, and water conservation.

### 9.1.2. The development of sustainable finance definitions in China

China's has multiple policies and programmes in the area of green and climate finance, not limited to financial regulation. For instance, five pilot zones for green finance innovation were set up in 2017 in Guangdong, Huizhou, Jiangxi, Zhejiang and Xinjiang. In other regions, seven regional carbon market pilots also were launched in 2013 and 2014, and a national carbon market in 2017[1]. In terms of financial regulation, China has three main frameworks for green finance definitions. The core framework is the "Guiding catalogue for the green industry". Originally established in 2016 and updated in 2019, this framework is the joint production of seven ministries and related commissions. These include the NDRC (planning ministry), the Ministry of Finance, the Ministry of Environmental Protection, the People's Bank of China (PBOC, the central bank) and the financial regulators of respectively the banking sector (China Banking Regulatory Commission, CBRC), the securities sector (China Securities Regulatory Commission, CSRC) and the insurance sector (China Insurance Regulatory Commission, CIRC). For lending, the CBRC issued in 2012 and subsequent years green credit guidelines, key performance indicators for green credit and green credit statistics forms. For green bonds, the PBOC issued a "green bond endorsed project catalogue" in 2015, which is often referred to as "the Chinese green bond taxonomy". Those frameworks are reviewed below.

## 9.2. Objectives and scope

### *9.2.1. The Guiding catalogue for the green industry*

There is no official translation of the catalogue into English as yet. An unofficial summary translation was consulted. The summary consists of a list of eligible sectors and contains no metrics or thresholds. The catalogue is based on both industrial policies and environmental considerations. For instance, based on the summary, the catalogue indicates a list of "high priority" hydropower projects but does not use quantitative, technology-agnostic thresholds like the EU taxonomy does. The six categories of green industries listed in the catalogue are:

1. Manufacture of energy efficient equipment
2. Clean production industry
3. Clean energy industry
4. Industry of ecology and environment
5. Green upgrade of infrastructure
6. Green services

### *9.2.2. Green lending*

Banks are the main providers of green finance in China. At the end of 2017, total green lending from 21 major Chinese banks was RMB 8.3 trillion (USD 1.1 trillion), or about 9% of their total lending. The five major green lenders were China Development Bank, Industrial and Commercial Bank of China, Construction Bank of China, Agricultural Bank of China and Bank of China.

The banking regulator CBRC regulates green lending by commercial banks. Between 2012 and 2014, the CBRC issued green credit guidelines, Key Performance Indicators (KPIs) for implementing green credit, and green credit statistics forms. The green credit guidelines provide a full set of recommendations for banks to embed climate, environmental and social risks and opportunities in their governance, strategy, policy, and disclosures. All policy banks, state owned commercial banks, joint-stock commercial banks, and postal savings banks are required to report data to the CBRC (half-year frequency) using a template. The data reporting is declarative and it appears that no external verification is required. Annex IV of the KPIs for implementing green credit provides a "brown list" of four categories of non-compliant loans that must be reported: amounts of loans to enterprises in violation of environmental protection or safety regulation, enterprises with obsolete capacity to be eliminated or those presenting worker safety concerns.

A "green taxonomy" is provided in another template to be similarly filled by banks: the form on "statistics on credit to projects and services of environmental protection and emission reduction". The form does not request that the reporting bank has adopted a broader sustainability agenda. However, it includes a list of green sectors and requests associated emission reductions.

It is worth noting that the CBRC green lending criteria exclude fossil fuel lending, which is the not the case for the green bond regulation as outlined below.

### 9.2.3. Green bonds

#### *The green bond market in China*

China is one of the largest issuers of green bonds in the world. Taking into account bonds issued in China that comply with international green bond standards, according to the Climate Bonds Initiative (CBI), China was the second largest green bond issuer ~~in~~ 2019 with USD 31.3 billion issued, after the USA (USD 51.3 billion issued) (CBI, 2019[6]). USD 24.2bn of Chinese issuances of labelled green bonds were excluded from these figures because they were not in line with international green bond definitions. Chinese entities issue green bonds not just on the domestic market, but also in overseas markets. According to CBI, about USD 6.6 billion of offshore green bonds were issued by Chinese entities in 2017, representing one fifth of total green bond issuance by Chinese entities in that year. Conversely, China also has established a green "panda bond" market, where RMB denominated green bonds may be issued in China by a foreign entity. Commercial banks make up the largest portion of issuance, representing 60% of new issuance in 2018. Bond maturity is relatively short, with 59% of total 2018 issuance with maturity below 5 years. Most proceeds are allocated to low carbon transportation (33% of the use of proceeds of bonds issued in 2018) and renewable energy projects (28%). The PBOC allows green bonds issued by financial institutions to be used as collateral for low interest central bank loans, which gives financial institutions a strong incentive to issue green bonds. It must be noted that 50% of bond proceeds are allowed to be directed to repaying bank loans and investing in working capital, while the CBI standard sets a maximum of 5% for those uses of green bond proceeds. CBI excludes from its count of green bonds those where more than 5% of proceeds are used for general corporate working capital or general funding purposes. In 2019 such bonds represented 75% of all excluded deals, the majority of which were from Chinese issuers.

#### *Green bond regulation*

China's green bonds legislation consists of two main components: the 2016 Green Bond Catalogue regulating corporate bonds, provided by the NDRC, and the Green Bond Endorsed Project Catalogue issued by the Green Finance Committee of China Society of Finance and Banking (under PBOC), which regulates green bonds issued by financial institutions. As noted, the latter is generally referred to as the Chinese green bond taxonomy.

More relevant information is available for the PBOC Catalogue, and information is added below about the NDRC Catalogue where available.

The PBOC's China Green Bond Endorsed Project Catalogue (2015 Edition) (Green Finance Committee, 2015[7]) for green bonds issued by banks and other financial institutions is available online in an English translation provided by ICMA. It provides a taxonomy of eligible activities, divided into six categories (Level 1 Category) and 31 sub-categories (Level 2 Category), with detailed explanations and defining criteria. Criteria include references to National Industry Classification Codes. The approach to eligibility is multidimensional across several environmental objectives, in a similar vein as the EU Taxonomy which it pre-dated. The Catalogue states that it "must take multi-dimensional environmental benefits as the defining standard. Project definition should take special consideration of environmental benefits in GHG emission reduction, pollution reduction, resource conservation, ecological protection."

The following text from the Catalogue describes the basic principles to which it adheres:

- Conforming to national conditions: focusing on improving the ecological environment and easing resource pressure, and following the lead of national industrial policy at the current stage.
- Highlighting environmental benefits: supporting projects with marked environmental benefits and positive spill over effects.

- Being simple and clear: taking into account the fact that most of the capital market practitioners are non-environmental professionals, and thus employing definition and classification method that is easy to follow and operate.
- Making continuous adjustment: timely updating the Catalogue according to technological advancement, policy adjustment, standard updates and changes in resource and environmental conditions.
- In line with international practice: taking international standards and practices as reference to develop domestic definition and classification method, in order to facilitate international cooperation in green finance."

Level 1 and 2 Categories in this taxonomy are shown below:

## Table 9.1. China – financial institutions green bond taxonomy (PBOC/ICMA 2015)

| Level 1 Category | Level 2 Category |
|---|---|
| Energy savings | Industrial Energy Savings |
| | Energy Savings – Technology Improvement |
| | Sustainable buildings |
| | Energy Management Centre |
| | Urban and rural infrastructure Construction with energy saving efficiency |
| Pollution prevention and control | Pollution prevention and control |
| | Environmental Restoration Project |
| | Clean Utilization of coal |
| Resource conservation and recycling | Water saving and unconventional water use |
| | Redevelopment and integrated utilization of tailings and associated mine |
| | Recycling and utilization of industrial solid wastes, exhaust gas and effluent |
| | Recycling, processing and utilization of renewable resource |
| | Remanufacturing of electromechanical products |
| | Recycling and utilization of biomass resource |
| Clean Transportation | Railway transportation |
| | Urban rail transportation (light rail) |
| | Public urban and rural transportation (bus) |
| | Waterway transportation |
| | Clean fuel |
| | New energy automobile |
| | Internet application on transportation |
| Clean energy | Wind power generation |
| | Solar Photovoltaic Power Generation |
| | Smart Grid and energy internet |
| | Distributed energy resource |
| | Social Thermal application |
| | Hydropower generation |
| | Other new energy application |
| Ecological protection and climate change adaptation | Natural ecological protection and protective development of tourism resource |
| | Ecological agriculture, husbandry and fishery |
| | Forestry development |
| | Emergency Prevention and Control of disaster |

Both the PBOC and NDRC green definitions include some project types that would not necessarily be considered green under some other international definitions (e.g. the EU Taxonomy). These include:

- Nuclear power generation
- Gas power production with criteria related to storage and shipping
- "Clean production of oil" is eligible as well as flaring
- Retrofits to fossil fuel power stations and infrastructure used for transporting fossil fuels
- "Clean" coal , although there have been announcements by Chinese officials that clean coal would be taken off the list of projects eligible for green bond financing. What is referred to as "clean coal" by Chinese authorities is otherwise known as supercritical coal (EDF, 2020[8]), i.e. a modern coal fired power generation process that is more efficient than traditional coal-fired generation, emits 20% less carbon dioxide and divides by 7 and 10 respectively nitrogen and sulphur oxide emissions.
- Large-scale (>50 MW) hydropower electricity generation

## 9.3. Metrics and thresholds

Metrics (in terms of emission reductions), but not thresholds, are available for green lending. Neither metrics nor thresholds are readily available in English language for the PBOC green bond taxonomy, nor the guiding catalogue for green industry.

## 9.4. Outlook and next steps

The sustainable finance definitions and taxonomies in China are not fully aligned amongst themselves. A case in point is the inclusion of fossil fuel related projects for the PBOC green bond standard but not for green lending. According to one prominent professor of green finance in China, "... various departments have standards for green agriculture, green buildings, and green manufacturing and technology, but there is no coordination between them" (Yao, 2018[9]). The Chinese authorities are working on harmonizing definitions, taking the 2019 guiding catalogue for the green industry as a main point of reference. China is also supports efforts to harmonise sustainable finance definitions at the international level. China became a member of the International Platform on Sustainable Finance (IPSF) launched by the EC in September 2019 to encourage international coordination on the various sustainable finance definitions. One of the future possible topics for a specific working group of the IPSF would be to work on a closer alignment of the Chinese definitions and the EU taxonomy, including where possible metrics and thresholds. The European Investment Bank (EIB), together with China's Green Finance Committee (GFC), issued two "white papers" (EIB, 2017[10]) (EIB, 2018[11]) on mapping and comparing China's Green Bond Endorsed Project Catalogue and the Common Principles for Climate Mitigation Finance Tracking.

## References


CBI (2019), *https://www.climatebonds.net/files/reports/2019_annual_highlights-final.pdf.* [6]

EDF (2020), *https://www.edf.fr/groupe-edf/producteur-industriel/thermique/atouts/technologies-avancees/centrale-au-charbon-a-haut-rendement.* [8]

EIB (2018), *https://www.eib.org/en/press/all/2018-327-towards-a-common-language-in-green-finance-progress-is-made-at-cop24-in-katowice.* [11]

EIB (2017), *https://www.eib.org/attachments/press/white-paper-green-finance-common-language-eib-and-green-finance-committee.pdf.* [10]

Feng, Y. et al. (2013), "Environmental Pollution Liability Insurance in China: In Need of Strong Government Backing", *AMBIO*, Vol. 43/5, pp. 687-702, http://dx.doi.org/10.1007/s13280-013-0436-0. [1]

Green Finance Committee (2015), *http://greenfinance.org.cn/displaynews.php?cid=79&id=468.* [7]

OECD (2018), *OECD Business and Finance Outlook 2018*, OECD Publishing, Paris, https://dx.doi.org/10.1787/9789264298828-en. [5]

UNFCCC (2015), *https://www4.unfccc.int/sites/submissions/INDC/Submission%20Pages/submissions.aspx.* [2]

Vivid Economics (2019), *https://www.vivideconomics.com/wp-content/uploads/2019/09/Decarbonizing-the-Belt-and-Road-%E2%80%93Final-Report-English.pdf.* [4]

Wikipedia (2020), *https://en.wikipedia.org/wiki/Belt_and_Road_Initiative.* [3]

Yao, W. (2018), *https://www.lse.ac.uk/GranthamInstitute/news/chinas-green-finance-strategy-much-achieved-further-to-go/.* [9]


## Notes

[1] The national trading programme is still in the implementation phase and as of 2019, the first trade was anticipated to take place in 2020.

# 10 Sustainable finance definitions in France

Sustainable finance definitions appear in the GreenFin label for investment funds, based on the Climate Bonds Initiative market-based taxonomy. In addition, the French State issued a sovereign green bond, which for the purpose of this analysis, is considered to contain official sustainable finance definitions.

## 10.1. Introduction

France was the first country to issue a sovereign green bond in 2017. France does not have a sustainable finance taxonomy per se. However, sustainable finance definitions appear in four pieces of legislation: the Green Fin and ISR labels for investment funds, the PACTE legislation and the "Article 173' of the 2015 Law of Energy Transition and Green Growth (LTECV). The Green Fin label for investment funds is based on the Climate Bonds Initiative taxonomy.

## 10.2. The French Sovereign Green Bond

### *10.2.1. Amount and objectives*

In January 2017, France launched its first sovereign green bond (Green OAT, Obligation Assimilable du Trésor). Since then, subsequent issues were made on the same tranche. The total outstanding amount was EUR 20.5 billion in March 2020, which makes it the largest green sovereign green bond in the world. Four objectives are identified in the Green OAT framework (République Française, 2017[1]): climate change mitigation (55% of the 2018 allocation), adaptation (25%), biodiversity (15%) and pollution (5%).

### *10.2.2. Verification*

As per the Green OAT Framework, the French State Treasury Agency (Agence France Trésor) issued yearly allocation and performance reports for 2017 and 2018. Auditing firm KPMG provided a reasonable assurance report on the allocation of proceeds. Second opinion provider Vigeo Eiris confirmed that the proceeds from the Green OAT had been used to fund green initiatives and that France had fulfilled its commitment under the Green OAT framework. An independent Green Bond Evaluation Council defines the guidelines and the frequency of the environmental impact reporting that would be most appropriate for each allocated expenditure. The OECD sits on this Council. In November 2018, the Green OAT Evaluation Council supervised a specific report related to the tax credit for energy transition (Crédit d'Impôt pour la Transition Energétique, CITE) (see below).

### *10.2.3. Use of proceeds*

France's Green OAT funds central government budget expenditure, and expenditure under the "Invest for the Future" programme (Programme pour les Investissements d'Avenir, PIA). Proceeds are managed like those of a conventional sovereign bond, with allocations to eligible green expenditure tracked and reported. More than 50% of allocations need to relate to current or future years' expenditures. Eligible green expenditure projects are identified ex ante by an inter-ministerial working group which reports to the Prime Minister. Projects need to be aligned with the criteria for the Green Fin Label (see below), which itself is based on the Climate Bonds Standard (the taxonomy of the Climate Bonds Initiative (CBI)). Expenditure must relate to one of the following six sectors: buildings, transport, energy (including smart grids), living resources, adaptation, pollution control and eco-efficiency. Nuclear, armament and all expenditure dedicated to fossil fuels are excluded.

#### *Buildings*

The bulk of the € 1.9 billion allocated to buildings was the €1.6 billion in funding allocated to the energy transition tax credit (CITE). The CITE accounted for one-third of the total 2017-2018 allocation.

The CITE is a 30% tax credit that households can claim in the year after carrying out energy performance renovations in their homes. Eligible renovations are capped at 8 000 euros for a single person and 16 000 euros for a couple. Eligible equipment and material must meet minimum technical criteria regarding energy efficiency. The company carrying out the work must be accredited under a domestic label called RGE, “Reconnu Garant de l’Environnement” (Service Public, 2019[2]). Two-thirds of the tax credits that were claimed were associated with insulation work. Seventy five thousand homes were renovated using the CITE during each of the years 2015 and 2016, equivalent to a 16% increase in annual investments in energy performance renovations. The renovations financed with a CITE are expected to reduce the energy consumption and the $CO_2$ emissions of the residential sector by roughly 7% of the 2015 level over the period 2015 to 2050.

The green OAT also served to refinance € 42 million of interest-free green loans. These loans are provided under French law by low-income mortgage intermediary SGFGAS, Société de Gestion des Financement et de la Garantie de l’Accession Sociale à la propriété (SGFGAS, 2019[3]) , which provides up to € 30 000 in zero-interest-rate loans to fund renovation that improves energy efficiency. This company acts as an intermediary between the French State and lending banks.

*Living resources (biodiversity)*

France is one of the ten countries with the highest number of endangered species (1 235 in total, of which 293 in mainland France)[1]. At € 772 million, “living resources” was the second largest item in terms of green OAT expenditure in 2018. The bulk of the allocation (€ 385 million) supported research, while € 226 million supported sustainable forest management best practices. Maintenance and extension of protected areas received € 125 million, while € 36 million was allocated to organic farming and biodiversity restoration on farms.

*Transport*

Transport has the highest greenhouse gas emissions of any sector in France (29% of 2016 emissions), mostly due to road transport. Green OAT proceeds focussed on three areas: vehicle energy efficiency and fuel carbon intensity (mostly through research programme CEREMA (CEREMA, 2020[4])), and modal shift, mostly through river equipment (€ 210 million to Voies Navigables de France (VNF, 2020[5])).

*Energy*

Of the € 376 million of 2018 proceeds going to energy, € 184 million went to public research.

*Adaptation*

Research expenditure, for observation of the Earth in support of climate change adaptation, accounted for € 775 million of proceeds from the green OAT in 2018.

*Pollution*

The French Senate has estimated the economic and financial cost of air pollution at between € 70 and 100 billion per year[2]. Against the backdrop of relevant European directives, France has pledged to achieve the following percentage reductions in emissions by 2030 compared to 2005 levels: $SO_2$ (77%), $NO_x$ (69%), non-methane volatile organic compounds (52%), particulate matter (57%), and ammonia (13%). The € 43 million devoted to pollution went to public research and studies.

### 10.2.4. Indicators

The OAT framework mentions that both output and impact indicators will be provided, and gives concrete examples. There are no thresholds indicated.

Performance against some 40 output indicators is assessed for categories of allocated expenditures, with levels reached in 2016, 2017 and 2018. A selection of indicators is presented below for the largest 2018 expenditures:

- Maintenance of French waterways: waterway availability rate (98% in 2018)
- CITE Energy renovation tax credit: number of households benefitting from the tax credit in thoushands ( 1202 in 2018)
- Environmental public research: Research produced by the programmes operators in the European Union: 6,2% in 2018

## 10.3. Objectives and scope of sustainable finance definitions in France

Apart from the Green OAT, four pieces of French legislation include sustainable finance definitions. They are the Green Fin and ISR labels for investment funds, the Loi PACTE (Plan d'Action pour la Croissance et la Transformation de l'Entreprise, or law for the Action Plan for Business Growth and Transformation) and the "Article 173" disclosure regulation (Article 173 of the 2015 Law of Energy Transition and Green Growth (LTECV)).

### *10.3.1. Green Fin label*

The Green Fin Label (formerly Energy and Ecological Transition for Climate, TEEC), was legally established in December 2015. It is administered by the Ministry of Ecology and Inclusive Transition, MTES, through three intermediary consulting companies, who act as verifiers of the label: Novethic (a branch of the national development bank Caisse des Dépôts et Consignations), Afnor and Ernst & Young (EY) France. The label gives a "green" tag to investment funds provided their portfolio meets the requirements. In total, 40 investment funds were labelled so far with total assets under management of € 11.5 billion (Label GreenFin, 2019[6]). Eligible funds are private equity funds, bond funds and real estate funds. Funds are eligible to use the label when they meet the following criteria:

- A certain percentage of their assets under management is invested in "green activities"
- Their investment respects exclusion criteria (fossil fuels and nuclear-related activities)
- They actively manage any Environmental, Social and Governance controversy that arises
- They measure and report their environmental impacts.

"Green activities" are defined with reference to the Climate Bonds Initiative taxonomy. The label defines three types of issuers whose securities (shares or bonds) or debt can be included in an investment fund:

- Type 1 issuers: 50 to 100% of their turnover comes from a green activity
- Type 2 issuers: 10 to 50% of their turnover comes from a green activity
- Type 3 issuers: 0 to 10% of turnover from a green activity.

For each category of investment funds, minimum thresholds between the three types of holdings are set. For instance, to be eligible to use the label, a private equity fund needs to have more than 75% of its assets invested in Type 1 issuers. Bond funds need to hold a minimum of 75% of their assets under management in green bonds that comply with the Green Bond Principles, which were developed by members of the financial industry and whose Executive Committee is co-ordinated by ICMA.

### *10.3.2. The ISR Label*

The Investissement Socialement Responsible (ISR) label was created by a 2016 legislation (Association Française de Gestion, 2019[7]). It provides recognition that an asset manager is using Environmental,

Social and Governance (ESG) criteria in their investment strategy. The label doesn't employ a taxonomy, metrics or thresholds. Instead, ESG criteria and management needs to be recognised by an external ESG verifier. The asset manager also needs to demonstrate that the shareholders of the investment funds in which the asset manager invests are actively engaging with investee companies. The label is audited by Afnor and EY France. Forty-five asset managers and 210 investment funds had received the label as of May 2019, for a total of assets under management of € 54 billion.

### *10.3.3. The PACTE Law (Plan d'action pour la croissance et la transformation des entreprises)*

The PACTE legislation was adopted in May 2019. It amended the French Insurance code (article 1 131-1-2). The legislation makes it mandatory for life insurance product providers to propose to investors at least one investment with the ISR or Green Fin label, or with at least 5 to 10% of its assets invested in securities from issuers belonging to the Social and Inclusive Economy sector (ESS), as defined by the French Labour Code (Code du Travail article L 333 – 2 – 17 -1). The Social and Inclusive Economy Sector (ESS in French) contains a variety of finance institutions, corporates and SMEs organised as cooperatives, mutual companies (« mutuelles »), associations, foundations, when their business and operations are based on principles of solidarity and societal goals (Ministère de l'Economie, 2020[8]).

## 10.4. Metrics and thresholds

The one French programme with clearly established definitions is the Green Fin label, which uses Climate Bond Initiative definitions (the Climate Bond Standards).

## 10.5. Outlook and next steps

During the fifth annual Climate Finance Day in Paris on November 29 2019, the French Finance Minister mentioned France supporting the implementation of the EU taxonomy by French financial actors as soon as 2021.

## References

Association Française de Gestion (2019), *https://www.afg.asso.fr/solutions-depargne/presentation-isr/label-isr/*. [7]

CEREMA (2020), *https://www.cerema.fr/fr*. [4]

Label GreenFin (2019), *https://www.ecologique-solidaire.gouv.fr/label-greenfin.*. [6]

Ministère de l'Economie (2020), *https://www.economie.gouv.fr/cedef/economie-sociale-et-solidaire*. [8]

République Française (2017), *https://aft.gouv.fr/files/archives/attachments/25562.pdf*. [1]

Service Public (2019), *https://www.service-public.fr/professionnels-entreprises/vosdroits/F32251*. [2]

SGFGAS (2019), *https://www2.sgfgas.fr/*. [3]

VNF (2020), *https://www.vnf.fr/vnf/accueil/qui-sommes-nous-vnf/*. [5]

## Notes

[1] Oat allocation report 2018, p 38

[2] Oat allocation report 2018, p 56

# 11 Sustainable finance definitions in the Netherlands

The Dutch State issued a sovereign green bond. In addition, the country has a long history of developing green finance products such as green loans, green mortgages and green funds.

## 11.1. Introduction

The Netherlands has developed sustainable finance definitions in three separate programmes, but no over-arching taxonomy. The definitions contain mostly principles. Metrics and thresholds could be identified only insofar as they refer to EU legislation (such as the Nearly Zero-Energy Buildings Directive, NZEB) or the CBI taxonomy (in the case of the Dutch sovereign green bond).

The Netherlands has been a pioneer in fostering greater consideration of climate risks in the financial system. In 2016, the Dutch Central Bank (De Nederlandsche Bank – DNB) established the Sustainable Finance Platform. It was set to promote and increase awareness of sustainable funding in the financial sector. DNB jointly founded the international Network (of central banks and financial regulators) on Greening the Financial System (NGFS), which is chaired by a member of the DNB Governing Board. De Nederlandsche Bank also was the first Central Bank to sign the UN Principles on Responsible Investment (PRI). In addition, the state-supported green investment vehicle Invest-NL was launched in 2020 with a capital of € 1.7 billion.

Cumulative Dutch green bond issuance in the fifteen months 2014-Q1 2018 period (therefore excluding the Sovereign Bond discussed below) was € 13 billion, and included eight issuers. The largest issuer was the energy grid Tennet with € 5 billion issued. The next largest was € 3.7 billion from the Nederlandse Waterschapsbank NV for, a dedicated lender which provides loans to the regional Water Boards. Commercial banks ING, ABN Amro and Rabobank, each issued green bonds of around of € 1 billion.

Sustainable finance definitions in the Netherlands were developed in the context of the following activities and programmes:

- Sovereign Green Bond: issued in 2019.
- Green funds scheme: used for various retail projects, mostly organic farming, greenhouses, and renewable energy.
- Green mortgages scheme: for energy performance improvements of buildings.

The Government supports the two latter instruments with financial incentives, which are further described below.

## 11.2. The Dutch Sovereign Green Bond

In May 2019, the Netherlands became the first AAA rated sovereign issuer to issue a green bond. The demand for the bond in capital markets was high, with orders amounting to more than three times the final allocation of € 5.98 billion.[1] The volume is to be increased through a later issuance towards a target of € 10 billion. The Dutch State Treasury Agency has committed to report on the allocation of funds raised and to perform an impact analysis of the proceeds. The bond was certified by CBI as meeting their Climate Bonds Standard, based on a pre-issuance verification letter by verifier Sustainalytics.

As described in the green bond framework (Green Bond Framework, 2019[1]) associated with the sovereign green bond, the bond will be invested in solar and marine renewable energy, low carbon land transportation, water infrastructure for climate change adaptation, and thermal insulation of property. Eligible green expenditures include such government expenditures as direct investment, subsidies, tax credits, and selected operational expenditures. Eligibility is limited to Central Government Budget expenditures in the budget year preceding the issuance, the budget year of the issuance and future budget years.

*Renewable Energy*: Subsidies under the Central Government law "Stimulation of Sustainable Energy Production (SDE)". Energies in scope are solar, on shore and off shore wind (Central Budget, 2019[2]) [2] .

Expected impact indicators (i.e. metrics) are actual annual energy production (in MWh), and annual GHG emissions avoidance.

*Climate Change Adaptation and Sustainable Water Management*: Expenditures under the Dutch Delta Programme (Delta Programme, 2019[3]) to ensure flood risk management, freshwater supply, and spatial planning will be climate-proof and water-resilient. Eligible expenditures include reinforcing flood defences, monitoring and management of water levels and water distribution. Expected indicators are availability of flood defences (in percentage) and reduction of flood risk / frequency.

*Clean Transportation*: Expenditures for the development, maintenance and management of railway infrastructure, excluding dedicated freight railway infrastructure. Eligible expenditures include those related to upgrading trajectories for higher-frequency passenger rail travel, railway capacity management, bicycle parking space at rail stations, and linkages to other modes of public transportation (Central Budget Art.13, 2019[4]). The expected indicator is annual passenger train kilometres.

*Energy efficiency*: Subsidies to housing corporations and property owners for the improvement of energy efficiency of residential homes in the rental sector via wall or floor insulation, high-efficiency glazing, more efficient central heating or other measures (Central Budget Art. 4, 2019[5]). Expected indicators are annual energy savings in MWh, annual GHG reduction.

## 11.3. Objectives and scope of sustainable finance definitions in the Netherlands

### *11.3.1. The Green Funds Scheme*

The "Green Funds Scheme" (Ministry of Housing, 2010[6]) has been in operation since 1995. It allows retail investors investing in qualifying green investments to benefit from tax relief, and allows eligible green projects to benefit from lower rates on bank loans. It also allows banks to establish green funds to finance those loans (see below). This scheme has channelled substantial amounts of retail savings to the financing of green projects in the Netherlands. The Green Funds Scheme is operated by four Ministries working closely together: Housing/Spatial Planning/Environment, which coordinates the whole scheme, Agriculture/Nature/Food Quality, Transport, Public Works/Water Management, and Finance. The Scheme comprises a Green Project Scheme (which sets the conditions for a project to be considered green) and a Green Institution Scheme (which regulates the role played by financial institutions), plus a tax incentive for individual investors.

#### *Green Projects*

Green projects should provide a significant and immediate environmental benefit. The seven categories are defined by law with the latest revision dating from March 30 2016[3]. They are:

- *Nature, forest and landscape* – protected zones including green zones in cities, wildlife tunnels, nest protection;
- *Agriculture* - organic farming, environmentally friendly horticultural greenhouses;
- *Energy* – wind turbines, solar cells, hydropower, heat pumps, LED lamps, waste heat;
- *Sustainable construction* – energy and water efficiency, construction from environmentally friendly materials;
- *Sustainable mobility* – cycle paths and parks, green public transport, cleaner inland ships.

#### *Green Institutions*

Several financial institutions have been recognised under the scheme as green banks[4], after indicating their willingness and ability to participate in the scheme. They are: ABN Amro, BNP Paribas Fortis, ING,

Rabobank, Triodos, ASN, National Groenfonds, and Stichting NOTS Re Investment. Banks offer low-cost loans to eligible companies/projects, and provide below average returns to retail consumers, but those below average returns are offset by a capital tax exemption. The banks issue fixed term bonds, or shares in a green investment fund. The cost paid to the market is lower than the standard market rate, which in turns allows the bank to fund projects at a cheaper rate.

*Tax incentive for individual investors*

Capital invested in an eligible green investment by an individual is tax exempt up to about 55 000 euros per person, instead of being subject to a regular 1,2% capital gains tax in the Netherlands. In addition, income from such investments receives a tax reduction of 1,3%. Individuals may invest either in a green fund or in a green savings account. The bank must invest at least 70% of the money in green projects. The bank provides a lower interest rate than the market rate, but this is compensated by the tax savings.

*Procedure and control*

The bank carries out an economic assessment of projects and applies to the Government for a Green Certificate if the project is a promising candidate under the Green Funds Scheme. The government checks the criteria and issues a certificate valid for 10 years if the project meets the criteria.

*Outcomes of the Green Funds Scheme*

According to the data in the brochure from the Ministry of Housing, Spatial Planning and the Environment (see note 8), over 14 years from 1995 to 2009, a cumulative total of € 7.4 billion euros was collected by the scheme, from 250 000 individual investors. One out of seven individual investors in the Netherlands holds a green bond or a share in a green fund. The average investor has invested € 30,000. Some 6000 projects were financed, with an average amount of 4 million euros per project. The most popular projects in terms of number of green certificates received have been organic farming, Green Label Greenhouses, and renewable energy. More than 800 million euros have been invested in organic farming, more than 1700 square kilometres of wood and nature conservation areas have been created in a decade, and one third of all greenhouses in the Netherlands have been brought up to the Green Label Greenhouse standard, which gets tighter every year.

A 2013 study by a Dutch consultancy (CE DELFT, 2013[7]) provided a cost-benefit assessment of the Green Funds Scheme. It concluded that the scheme was successful in improving the business case for innovative sustainable projects, and at channelling capital to those projects, in a cost effective manner.

### 11.3.2. The Green Mortgage Scheme

*Residential building energy performance standards: The National Energy Act (2013) and the Energy Agenda (2016)*

Energy performance standards for residential buildings have been in effect since 1995 in the Netherlands (RVO, 2016[8]). Following the implementation of the European Directive 201/31/EU on the Energy Performance of Buildings, owners of residential buildings are required to obtain an Energy Performance Certificate or Label ranking from A (best) to G (worst). In 2013, the National Energy Act was established, with three objectives:

- by 2020, achieve an upgrade (equivalent to two levels in the Energy Label rankings) for 300 000 residences
- renovate the social housing building stock to an average of energy class B
- improve 80% of the private rented houses to a minimum of energy class C.

In 2016, an "Energy Agenda" was signed, establishing objectives to 2050, including phasing out offices and rented houses with an energy label worse than C, and gradually reducing the use of natural gas in the built environment. In addition, according to the European Directive, all newly built houses after 2020 need to reach NZEB - Nearly Zero Energy Buildings.

### *The Energy Performance Coefficient*

The main requirement for the energy performance of new buildings is the Energy Performance Coefficient (EPC). The EPC is the quotient obtained by dividing a building's calculated primary energy needs by the allowed primary energy performance, measured in mJ/m², or milliJoules per square meter. The coefficient is therefore unitless. Primary energy needs and performance are estimated based on a series of indicators, e.g. heating, ventilation and lighting, adjusted according to the useful floor area and the renewable energy produced by the building. There are also legal requirements for the thermal quality of the building envelope for new buildings and major renovations (i.e. concerning more than 25% of the envelope), measured in R-value for walls, roof and floor (m2 .K/W), or U value for windows and doors (W/m2.K).

### *Gradual decrease of the EPC*

The calculation of the EPC is mandatory for all new buildings and for large renovations in houses and offices. Municipalities have the legal power to halt construction projects if there is no compliance with the legal requirements for EPC. EPC requirements are set by building type (e.g. 1.8 for a hospital and 0.4 for a residential building in 2016. The latter figure is roughly equivalent to 50 to 65 kWh/m2 a year), and is gradually lowered for new buildings so as to reach NZEB in 2020.

### *Cheaper "green" mortgages*

Purchases of new houses or renovations by owner-occupiers are eligible for green certificates if energy-saving measures are implemented and lead to an improvement of the energy index by:

- At least 0.6 to a maximum of 1.4 (category 9d.1)
- At least 1.3 to a maximum of 1.4 (category 9d.2)
- At least 1.5 to a maximum of 1.2 (category 9d.3)
- To energy index 0 (category 9d.4)

Based on home renovation plans and documents demonstrating the requisite energy performance improvement, a bank can offer a green loan or mortgage with an interest rate that is below the normal interest rate. The maximum amount of the reduced rate mortgage is set from € 25 k to € 100k based on the categories above. The interest rate reduction is in the range of 25% below the normal interest rate and depends on a complex formula.

### *Outcomes of the Green Mortgage Scheme*

The total amount of mortgages outstanding in the Netherlands was € 600 billion as of end 2018[5]. Based on a poll of 1588 respondents organised by DNB (DNB, 2017[9]) homeowners mainly use their savings to finance investments to green their homes. In the period 1997-2017, 45% of homeowners invested in making their home more energy efficient (via insulation or sustainable energy). Only 4% financed these investments by means of bank loans. Of the households not making investments to green their homes, only 1.4% said this was due to their not being able to get a bank loan. More frequently stated reasons include a lack of savings and aversion to run up debt. High installation costs, and difficulties in comparing costs and benefits were also cited.

## 11.4. Metrics and thresholds Sovereign Green Bond

The Sovereign Bond framework explicitly refers to CBI criteria for renewable energy.

### *11.4.1. Green Funds Scheme*

There are no other metrics and thresholds that the ones presented above in legislation. Projects are assessed and approved by the relevant Ministries, upon submission by the banks (see graph above). This is consistent with the retail nature of projects.

### *11.4.2. Green Mortgage Scheme*

The metrics and thresholds in terms of energy performance coefficient and energy index are consistent with the European NZEB Directive.

## 11.5. Outlook and next steps

There is no specific initiative in the Netherlands on sustainable finance definitions and taxonomies at the time of writing.

## References


CE DELFT (2013), *https://www.cedelft.eu/en/publications/1408/the-environmental-and-economic-benefits-of-the-dutch-green-financing-scheme.* [11]

CE DELFT (2013), *https://www.cedelft.eu/en/publications/1408/the-environmental-and-economic-benefits-of-the-dutch-green-financing-scheme.* [7]

Central Budget (2019), *http://www.rijksbegroting.nl/2019/voorbereiding/begroting,kst248548_15.html.* [2]

Central Budget Art. 4 (2019), *http://www.rijksbegroting.nl/2019/voorbereiding/begroting,kst248515_9.html.* [5]

Central Budget Art.13 (2019), *http://www.rijksbegroting.nl/2019/voorbereiding/begroting,kst248451_7.html.* [4]

Delta Programme (2019), *https://www.government.nl/topics/delta-programme.* [3]

DNB (2017), *https://www.dnb.nl/en/news/news-and-archive/dnbulletin-2017/index.jsp.* [9]

Green Bond Framework (2019), *https://zoek.officielebekendmakingen.nl/blg-879136.pdf.* [1]

Ministry of Housing (2010), *https://www.rvo.nl/sites/default/files/bijlagen/SEN040%20DOW%20A4%20Greenfunds_tcm24-119449.pdf.* [6]

OECD (2016), *Green Investment Banks: Scaling up Private Investment in Low-carbon, Climate-resilient Infrastructure*, Green Finance and Investment, OECD Publishing, Paris, https://dx.doi.org/10.1787/9789264245129-en. [10]

RVO (2016), *https://epbd-ca.eu/ca-outcomes/outcomes-2015-2018/book-2018/countries/netherlands.* [8]


## Notes

[1] France's initial sovereign green bond issuance (€ 7 billion) in 2017 had a similar level of over-subscription; http://www.climateaction.org/news/record_7.5_billion_in_green_bonds_issued_by_france .

[2] Eligibility is limited to technologies for which Climate Bonds Initiative sector criteria are available, currently solar energy and onshore and offshore wind energy.

[3] See Staatscourant Nr 15 992 31 March 2016, Regeling GroenProjecten 2016, legislation number IENM/BSK 2015/ 209791.

[4] Green banks in this context are distinct from (public) green investment banks, which are publicly capitalised entity established specifically to facilitate private investment into domestic low-carbon, climate-resilient infrastructure and other green sectors such as water and waste management Paris (OECD, 2016[10]) .

[5] Source: DNB Dashboard

www.ingramcontent.com/pod-product-compliance
Ingram Content Group UK Ltd.
Pitfield, Milton Keynes, MK11 3LW, UK
UKHW051505290926
15471UKWH00008B/1426